An Invitation to explore the Viaducts of our Minds

Europäische Hochschulschriften

European University Studies

Publications Universitaires Européennes

Reihe XIV **Angelsächsische Sprache und Literatur**

Series XIV Anglo-Saxon Language and Literature

Série XIV Langue et littérature anglo-saxonnes

Band/Volume **472**

Sandra Schenk

An Invitation to explore the Viaducts of our Minds

Ideology Critique in American Literature and Film during the Seventies

Bibliographic Information published by the Deutsche Nationalbibliothek
The Deutsche Nationalbibliothek lists this publication in the Deutsche Nationalbibliografie; detailed bibliographic data is available in the internet at http://dnb.d-nb.de.

ISSN 0721-3387
ISBN 978-3-631-65150-6 (Print)
E-ISBN 978-3-653-04364-8 (E-Book)
DOI 10.3726/978-3-653-04364-8

PL Academic Research is an Imprint of Peter Lang GmbH.
Peter Lang – Frankfurt am Main · Bern · Bruxelles · New York · Oxford · Warszawa · Wien

This book was peer reviewed prior to publication.

www.peterlang.com

Dedicated to

Wes Craven, Peter Watkins, Hubert Selby, Jr., & Philip K. Dick, Gustav Hasford, George A. Romero who explored the dark spaces of the American experience and thus created spiritual guidance.

Preface

To carry death in your smile is *pornographic violence . . .*

The 1970s are a fascinating and in terms of cultural turbulences an eminently virulent era. In the progression from modernity to postmodernity, the decade is a somewhat neglected phase that is too often taken to be merely 'transitional.' In this neglect, it resembles the 30s and 40s, which lie, similarly forgotten, between the high modernism of the 20s and the rise of the suburban dispositifs and lifestyles in the 50s that will spill over into the 60s counter-culture. The 70s mark a similar gap, lying between the 60s, whose ideals are the exact opposite of a global capitalism and a similarly global hedonism promoted during the 80s.

In-between these decades, whose complexities and paradoxes have been charted in great detail, the 70s form, again like the 30s and 40s, a kind of cultural 'terrain vague;' a weirdly empty space lying in-between more clearly defined areas. Still, these forgotten cultural terrains were in many ways crucial. If the main inventions of the 30s were various forms of plastic, those of the 70s had to do with new media, such as the floppy disk, the liquid-crystal display, the videocassette, the cellphone and the walkman, as well as with the body, such as aesthetic protocols from early aerobics to liposuction.

It is with the full force of contemporary theory – ranging from Jacques Lacan, Jean Baudrillard, Roland Barthes, Michel Foucault, Walter Benjamin, Paul de Man, Julia Kristeva, Pierre Bourdieu, to Gilles Deleuze and Marshall McLuhan – that Schenk, in *An Invitation to explore the Viaducts of our Minds: Ideology Critique in American Literature and Film during the Seventies* enters this eerie, often uncannily familiar landscape, analyzing artistic practices that put into writing or onto the screen frightening figures of the relation between power and the body. The result is an extremely impressive panorama, as fascinating as it is scary, of an America that assembles, as if it were on a secret, or perhaps unconscious suicide mission, all of the ingredients of its present-day predicaments.

With an astonishing breadth of vision and an impressive depth of engagement, Schenk provides a cartography of this 'terrain vague,' engaging with the work of artists such as Wes Craven, Hubert Selby Jr., Peter Watkins, Philip K.

Dick, Gustav Hasford and Georg A. Romero, with a bit of J.G. Ballard thrown in for extra effect.

Prof. Dr. Hanjo Berressem
April 2014

Contents

An Invitation to Explore the Viaducts of our Minds: Ideology Critique in American Literature and Film during the Seventies

La Couleur du Temps

> L'art feuillette les siècles, feuillette la nature, interroge les chroniques, s'étudie à reproduire la réalité des faits, surtout celle des mœurs et des caractères, bien moins léguée au doute et à la contradiction que les faits, restaure ce que les annalistes ont tronqué, harmonise ce qu'ils ont dépareillé, devine leurs *omissions* et les répare, comble leurs *lacunes* par des imaginations qui aient la *couleur du temps*, groupe ce qu'ils ont laissé épars, rétablit le jeu des fils de la providence sous les marionnettes humaines, revêt le tout d'une forme poétique et naturelle à la fois, et lui donne cette vie de vérité et de saillie qui enfante l'illusion, ce *prestige de réalité* qui passionne le spectateur, et le poète, car le poète est de bonne foi. Ainsi le but de l'art est presque divin: ressusciter, s'il fait de l'histoire; *créer*, s'il fait de la poésie.[1]

Victor Hugo's famous preface to *Cromwell*, which developed into a manifest on Romanticism, still has an enormous impact on how to perceive art in general. There is a timelessness about his writing that transcends time and literary movements. The key terms of relevance for this thesis are *omissions, lacunes, couleur du temps,* and *prestige de réalité*. Hugo outlines the color of a particular time should not only be visible on the surface of a work of art but it should be infused with it.[2] Within the focus of this interrogation are American literature and film during the seventies. Henry Miller once wrote that America does not

---

1 {see Victor Hugo, Cromwell (Paris 1990), pp. 90-91. [italics mine] "Art leafs through the centuries and through nature. Art studies history and tries to reproduce the reality of facts but primarily the reality of morality and character. Art is invested in doubt and contradiction and restores what historians have disfigured as well as harmonizes what they have fragmented. Art conjectures their omission and mends them, it fills the gap with the power of imagination which has the color of the time. Art combines what they have left scattered and reconstructs the game of providence with human puppets. Art conceptualizes all this in a form that is poetic as well as natural. It gives this form a life of authenticity and observation which produces an illusion. This prestige of reality fascinates the audience and the naïve poet. Thus the aim of art is almost divine: history revives whereas poetry creates. [trans. mine]}

2 {see Hugo, Cromwell, p. 91}

exist. “It's a name you give to an abstract idea...”[3] America as an abstract idea is created out of the imagination of artists who focus on the dark side of the American experience. Christopher Priest describes in his novel *The Prestige* the three stages of illusion. The third stage is the effect or the prestige, which is the product of magic. One category of the magical trick is the production that consists of the creation of something out of nothing.[4] The combination of Priest's metafictional reflexivity with Hugo's idea of an illusion he terms *prestige de réalité* leads back to Millers non-existing America. Art has to create what has been omitted, it has to imagine the blank spaces of history or the abstract idea itself. From a Marxist perspective literature must be understood in relation to historical and social reality. Georg Lukács argues literary works reproduce the dominant ideologies of their time and they incorporate in their very form a critique of these ideologies.[5] The basic foundation of this argument is that art is not created in a social void but bears the mark of time and place. Historical reality (place) refers to an American context and social reality (time) refers to a particular point in time. The works of art are analyzed with special regard to historical and social reality under the influence of ideology. Ideology blinds us to our own conditions of life and misrepresents the world to ourselves. In Marxist usage, ideology makes us experience our life in ways that make us believe the way we perceive ourselves and the world is natural. Ideology *dis*torts reality and renders what is actually artificial and contradictory as natural and harmonious. Marxism describes submission to ideology as a state of false consciousness.[6] Louis Althusser argues ideology 'functions' in such a way that it 'transforms' the individuals into subjects by interpellation.[7] The *dis*tortion of reality and the mechanism of subjection are of special interest here. Ideology is a focal point here but there is no desire to restore 'the truth beneath the simulacrum.'[8] The spaces inhabited by the works of art under discussion are analyzed as allegorical spaces, or hyperreal spaces. Referentiality is not an illusion nurtured and certainty is not a mirage cherished within the range of this argument.

For Benjamin, the linking of disparate images becomes a constellation. A constellation of stars forms a fictitious unity with a certain truth value and thus

3 {see Henry Miller, The Obelisk Trilogy (Paris 2004), p. 102}

4 {see Christopher Priest, The Prestige (London 2006), pp. 64-65}

5 {see K. M. Newton, Twentieth-Century Literary Theory: A Reader (London 1988), p. 85}

6 {see Hans Bertens, Literary Theory: The Basics (London 2001), pp. 84-85}

7 {see Louis Althusser, On Ideology (New York 2008), p. 48}

8 {see Jean Baudrillard, Simulacra and Simulacrum (Ann Arbor 1997), p. 27 }

becomes an allegory. "The creation of a meaningful constellation is the same as the creation of allegory."[9] The aim of this argument is to create a constellation between six important works of art with focus on how power relations affect / transform bodies. "Thus the State never intentionally confronts a man's sense, intellectual or moral, but only his body, his senses."[10] Henry David Thoreau observes the body is the primary target of the State with the goal of control. For the auteur David Cronenberg the human body is the first fact of human existence.[11]

> Everything comes out of the body and the fact of human mortality. It's natural that my film would focus on that. [...] It's a discussion of the body. It's a discussion of human existence as a physical event and phenomenon. Then add to that the level of metaphor I like to deal with, and you get what I do... It protected me, the genre.[12]

Cronenberg connects the themes of human existence and how bodies are transformed with metaphor in order to create art. Metaphor as well as genre work together and form a combination, which protects his freedom as an auteur and also increases the enigmatic quality of his art. This also holds true for the works of art within the range of this argument. Michel Foucault offers some important insights into the mechanisms of power, which are relevant for this argument. Discipline is a type of power and comprises a whole set of instruments, techniques, procedures, levels of application, targets. Foucault outlines the historical moment of the disciplines was the moment when an art of the human body was born. This art was directed at the formation of a relation whose very mechanism makes the human body more obedient in the event of making it more useful. The human body was introduced to a machinery of power, which broke it down and rearranged it.[13] The key phrases here are '*an art of the human body*' and '*machinery of power.*' What kind of mechanism does emerge in the works under discussion and what kind of connection can be established between the works? Foucault recommends to study power with focus on *how relations of subjuga-*

---

9 {see Jeremy Tambling, Allegory (New York 2010), pp. 120-121}

10 {see Henry David Thoreau, Civil Disobedience and other Essays (New York 1993), p. 12}

11 {see David Cronenberg and Serge Grünberg, David Cronenberg: Interviews with Serge Grünberg (London 2006), p. 39}

12 {see Cronenberg, David Cronenberg, pp. 39-40}

13 {see Michel Foucault, Discipline & Punish: The Birth of the Prison (New York 1995), pp. 215, 137-138}

tion can manufacture subjects.[14] The analysis of *relations of subjugation* is the main objective of this argument.

For Hugo, language is not fixed. The human spirit is in continuous motion and language as well. Every era has its very own ideas and its very own words to describe them. Language is like an ocean whose waves are in constant turmoil.[15] Language is an essential part of this argument and special focus is laid on the ideas, which define the seventies as well as the words used to describe them. Roland Barthes states a semiologist sees the sign moving in the field of signification. The semiologist has to enumerate the valences of the sign and traces their configuration. The sign is perceived as a *sensuous idea*. Each consciousness of the sign (symbolic, paradigmatic, and syntagmatic) corresponds to a certain moment of reflection, either individual or collective. A *'certain moment of reflection'* is of vital importance for this interrogation as the moment of emergence is regarded as crucial. According to Barthes, the syntagmatic consciousness unites signs on the level of discourse itself. It foresees the sign in its extension and is an imagination of the chain or the network. Barthes describes it further as an arrangement of mobile, substitutive parts whose combination *produces* meaning.[16] The aim of this argument is to establish a network of mobile parts between works of art in order to create a combination. This particular combination is perceived against the backdrop of historical and social reality with focus on *relations of subjugation*.

Meaning can be produced but as the parts are mobile there are innumerous constellations and consequently multiple meanings. Certainty is not an option.

> "My glimpse of an *unmoving world*, of the thousands of *drivers sitting passively* in their cars on the *motorway embankments* along the horizon, seemed to be a unique vision of this *machine landscape*, an invitation to explore the *viaducts of our minds*."[17]

J. G. Ballard describes his novel *Crash* as an extreme metaphor for an extreme situation, a kit of desperate measures only for use in an extreme crisis.[18] America during the seventies had to face extreme states of crisis and its very foundation was challenged. The unique language applied by Ballard serves as point of

14 {Michel Foucault, "Society must be defended": Lectures at the Collège de France, 1975-1976 (New York 2003), p. 265}

15 {see Hugo, Cromwell, p. 95}

16 {see Roland Barthes, Selected Writings (London 1983), pp. 212-213, 215- 217}

17 {see J. G. Ballard, Crash (London 2008), p. 40 [italics mine]}

18 {see Ballard, Crash, Introduction}

departure in order to illustrate a certain scenario: Artists exploring an unmoving / frozen world, traveling through machine landscapes and diving into the viaducts of minds as into an ocean. Like Ballard's language they dive into the gaps between the natural and the unnatural and hence illuminate the *lacunes* of history. They present us with the *prestige de réalité*.

Illuminer à la Fois l'Intérieur et l'Extérieur des Hommes

Misuse and Abuse of Authority

An Analysis of Sadistic Authorities

> A complete film-maker should be able to appeal to all facets of human existence. The sensual as well as the cerebral. If you do get this mixture together properly, you have a perfect example of healing the Cartesian schism. You have something that appeals to the intellect and to the viscera.[19]

« L'homme est double comme sa destinée, il y a en lui un animal et une intelligence, une âme et un corps; en un mot, il est le point d'intersection [...] » Hugo outlines the goal of art is to open up a double horizon for the spectator which illuminates the inside and the outside at the same time.[20] The similarity between Hugo's and Cronenberg's perception of the task of art is stunning as both share the same vision. The foundation of this argument is that art aims at healing the Cartesian schism whereas power seeks to keep it apart. This argument is partitioned in two sections and the first section explores the early seventies whereas the second section focuses on the late seventies. The three works discussed in the first section are Wes Craven's *The Last House on the Left*, Peter Watkins's *Punishment Park*, and Hubert Selby, Jr.'s *The Room*. The three works in the second section are Philip K. Dick's *A Scanner Darkly*, Gustav Hasford's *The Short-Timers* and George A. Romero's *Dawn of the Dead*. These six disparate works will be linked in order to create a constellation. They are analyzed as allegories, which examine bourgeois mythology and the effects of power on the body. In order to clarify the theoretical approach these three points are elaborated and their relevance with regard to this particular approach is illustrated. According to Robert Stam, the empty sequentiality of the post from postmodern corresponds to a preference for prefixes such as *de*-politicization or *dis*-location. These prefixes suggest the demystification of preexisting paradigms. One central leitmotif of postmodernism is the *de*substantialization of the subject, which de-

---

19 {see David Cronenberg, Cronenberg on Cronenberg (London 1997), p. 90}

20 {see Hugo, Cromwell, p. 66, 91. "Man and his destiny are both dual. Within man is an animal and an intelligence, a soul and a body. To put it in a nutshell, he is the point of intersection ..." [trans. mine]}

scribes the transmutation of the old, stable ego into a fractured, discursive construct, fashioned by the media and by social discourses. Two other vital leitmotifs are the *de*referentialization of the real and an atrophied historical sense.[21] *De*substantialization is tightly connected to power relations, *de*referentialization is read in context with allegory, and *the atrophied historical sense* is central for the construction of myths.

Focus is now laid on *de*referentialization and why it complements the concept of allegory. Jean Baudrillard outlines the era of simulation is inaugurated by a liquidation of all referentials who are resurrected in the systems of signs. It is no longer a question of imitation but of *substitution*. Signs of the real are *substituted* for the real, which is an operation of deterring every real process via its operational double. Representation is based on the principle of an equivalence of the sign and the real whereas simulation is based on the utopia of the very principle of equivalence. Simulation is a radical negation of the sign as value and envelops the whole edifice of representation itself as a simulacrum.[22] *Substitution* is the key word, which is of immense importance for the reasoning in question. Simulation is a space that is *substituted* and based on the principle of difference. Jacques Derrida outlines the sign represents the present in its absence. When a present cannot be stated then the sign takes the place of the present. The present is signified via the *detour of the sign*. The elements of signification function through the *network of oppositions* that distinguishes them and then relates them to one another. This condition of signification affects the totality of the sign, i. e. the signified and the signifier.[23] What cannot be presented or expressed has to be signified via the *detour of the sign*. Signification works in a *network of oppositions* and affects the relations of the sign. According to Saussure, the idea that a sign contains is of less importance than the other signs that surround it.[24] There is an intricate connection between the *network of oppositions* and the syntagmatic relation, between the outside and the inside of the sign. Bourdieu describes the construction of space as a necessary *detour* that is important to establish a *network structure*. This structure is a matrix of objective relations that link an agent to a collection of other agents in the same field who are facing the same

---

21 {see Robert Stam, Film Theory: An Introduction (Malden 2000), pp. 300-301}

22 {see Jean Baudrillard, Simularca and Simulation (Ann Arbor 1997), pp. 2, 6}

23 {see Paul Du Gay, Jessica Evans, Peter Redman, Identity: A Reader (London 2000), pp. 87-89}

24 {see Du Gay, Identity, p. 89}

realm of possibilities. [25] The works of art under discussion create allegorical spaces and thus are linked in the same realm of possibilities. Jeremy Tambling describes allegory as a rhetorical device within language, which exploits the gaps between words and meanings. The *dis*placement of language defines allegory as speaking one thing while implying another. For example, life as a journey means that a temporal process is *substituted* by a movement from place to place. A sustained and developed metaphor is an allegory, which makes abstract ideas appear powerful. It is an indicator of the impossibility of keeping an abstract concept or construction abstract. Thinking within figures of speech becomes allegorical and thus gives a visual or linguistic shape to those concepts and constructions. The conclusion is that the difference between the abstract and the visual or linguistic shape is effaced.[26] Allegory has its beginnings as a hallmark of theological certainty, but in its postmodern arrival it signals the retreat of such certainty.[27] *Substitution* is encountered as abstract concepts cannot be expressed, it is a necessary detour. The very process of *substitution* illustrates the arbitrary choice of a shape, which does not represent the abstract concept as it is inexpressible, i. e. there cannot be any referentiality. It is important to underline that allegory functions via the *de*referentialization of the real that is absent. Allegory and simulation are founded on the *principle of difference.* For Paul de Man, allegory originates in a *loss of reality*. The widening gulf between word (language) and object (world) produces a split between statement and meaning. Thus allegories exemplify the impossibility of naming. Benjamin and de Man regard language as non-representational as the real world cannot be described through language or decoded through a metalanguage.[28] Allegorical works invite repetition as they continually withdraw from the grasp of the reader (viewer). *De*referentialization is compelling as the lack of reality promises the work will continually transform itself and unfold only possibilities but no certainty.

How are allegory and ideology linked with each other? Tambling states symbolism is of great importance within any kind of ideology whether it is political or class- or gender-based. The symbol describes things as *natural*, which implies certain values are *natural* or have an unchanging existence. Ideology aims at stating that certain things are *natural* and Walter Benjamin argues ide-

25 {see Du Gay, Identity, p. 304}

26 {see Tambling, Allegory, pp. 3, 6, 12, 14, 171}

27 {see Copeland, Cambridge, p. 11}

28 {see Tambling, Allegory, pp. 129, 131, 134, 138-139, 165}

ology controls partly through the power of symbolism. Allegory disrupts the ruling of ideology and sanctions no idea of an originary record of unity. It focuses on the history that stands outside the chronological narrative of progress that makes up official history. All terms in allegory are *non-natural*, ideological, non-proper, catachreses. The allegorical image signifies a lack of representation and is only a fragment. Benjamin states allegories are ruins of thoughts that are internally self-divided. The allegorical image exemplifies that no unique value can be given to the object or its representation. He outlines the object represented has gone and is only present as an allegorical image.[29] Symbolism is connected to ideology and allegory is connected to ideology critique. Symbolism renders things as *natural* whereas allegory as substitution is itself *non-natural* due to its arbitrary shape. The focus on history that stands outside of official history is of central importance for the works within the range of this discussion. As so many events were covered-up and hidden from the public the works orbit around these *omissions*. They try to establish the *lacunes* and thus are founded on the very *lack of history*. The statement 'allegories are the natural mirrors of ideology'[30] sheds another light on the connection. Allegory as a mirror shows us the mechanism of ideology that lacks any real representation. Althusser describes ideology as a pure illusion, a nothingness whose reality is external to it. It is an imaginary construction.[31] Allegory and ideology both employ the detour of a construction of space and are founded on the *lack of reality*. Tambling suggests reading for allegory may be one way of finding new strategies of reading, which may open up new possibilities for interpretation.[32] This argument follows the idea that reading for allegory may open up new insights as the connection between allegory and ideology is such an important one and hence has to be taken into consideration. The American Marxist critic Fredric Jameson contends that writing always is linked with politics, which are beneath the surface of texts and appear within the text as symptoms. Jameson's political unconscious has a determinant referent and thus may be described as nostalgia for a single origin. Gayatari Spivak argues this produces allegory's most dangerous tendency, which is the search for an overarching meaning.[33] This poses the double bind of an allegorical reading and is the ultimate challenge for an allegorical reading as such.

---

29 {see Tambling, Allegory, pp. 116-120}

30 {see Tambling, Allegory, p. 170}

31 {see Althusser, On Ideology, p. 33}

32 {see Tambling, Allegory, p. 160}

33 {see Tambling, Allegory, p. 156}

Politics are beneath the surface of texts but allegory works as substitution for *omissions* and thus is constituted of the lack of a referent. This is the working assumption of this argument and hence the tendency of a search for a unified meaning is rejected. Jacques Lacan states if one wishes to deceive a man one has to *present* to him the painting of a *veil*. This incites a man to ask what is behind.[34] Allegory tends to make meaning *dis*appear behind a *veil*. Allegory conceals meaning.[35] *Veil* is an interesting term here as it brings us back to Priest and the metaphor of the magic trick. Priest writes the oldest axiom of magic is that the miracle of the trick must be made clear by the representation.[36] The *presentation of the veil* is crucial as it is an essential part of the deception. How the *dis*appearance is enacted is important for the trick.

Now the chain from allegory to ideology is extended to mythology. Roland Barthes describes myth as a system of communication, a mode of signification. Mythology has a historical foundation and comprises written discourse, photography, cinema etc. Pictures become a kind of writing as soon as they are meaningful. Mythical speech presupposes a signifying consciousness. Mythology is only one fragment of the vast science of signs that is semiology, which studies *signification apart from their content*. Mythology is part of semiology, formal science and of ideology as it studies ideas-in-form.[37] Mythology functions in a network, as signification cannot be derived from its content alone. It is linked to ideology as both give shape to abstract concepts. According to Barthes, mythology is based on the tri-dimensional pattern of the signifier, the signified, and the sign. It is constructed from a semiological chain that existed before and thus is a second-order semiological system. The sign in the linguistic system becomes a signifier in the mythical system. It is ambiguous as it is full on the one side (meaning) and empty on the other side (form). Meaning becomes impoverished when it turns into form, which is an abnormal regression from the linguistic sign to the mythical signifier. Myth turns signification into an empty parasitical form but it only puts meaning at a distance, it hides it.[38] Meaning is *veiled* through the abnormal regression from linguistic sign to mythical signifier. The act of impoverishment corresponds to the widening gulf between word (lan-

34 {see Oliver Harris, William Burroughs and the Secret of Fascination (Carbondale 2006), p. 1}

35 {see Tambling, Allegory, p. 164}

36 {see Priest, The Prestige, p. 286}

37 {see Roland Barthes, Barthes: Selected Writings (London 1983), pp.93-97}

38 {see Barthes, Barthes, pp. 99, 102-104}

guage) and object (world) in allegory. Both illustrate a split between statement and meaning.

Barthes states the form may be abstract but the concept is not, it is filled with a situation. *The concept is less reality than a knowledge of reality.* It is a chain of causes and effects, motives and intentions. A *repetition* of the concept through different forms allows the mythologist to decipher a myth because this insistent kind of behavior reveals its intentions.[39] The form is abstract whereas the concept is based on a *knowledge of reality* and thus the pursuit of a repetition of a concept can render insights into its motivation. Barthes further argues signification is the myth itself, which hides nothing but *dis*torts. Meaning is not abolished but alienated by the concept. Meaning and form are never at the same place and thus there is no contradiction between them. The form of the mythical signifier is empty but present, its meaning absent but full. Myth is defined by intention rather than by its literal sense but the intention is *frozen*, made absent by the literal sense. Myth plays on the analogy between meaning and form that is motivated. Motivation is unavoidable as well as *fragmentary.*[40] It can be concluded myth is a mode of signification that distorts. The absent meaning and present form are separated from each other and thus the presence of form is constituted on the absence of meaning. The mythical signifier is fragmented and thus ambivalent. Barthes outlines the duplicity of the signifier generates three different types of reading and the type of interest within the range of this argument is the third type. The focus is laid on the mythical signifier as a whole of meaning and form, an ambiguous signification. This type responds to the constituting mechanism of myth, its dynamics and thus perceives myth as true as well as *unreal*. In order to pass from semiology to ideology the third type of focusing must be utilized. When myth is driven either to *unveil* or to liquidate the concept, it will naturalize it. Myth transforms history into Nature.[41] The ambiguous signification is essential to the reading of myths and focus is laid on the gap between absence and presence in order to perceive myth as true as well as unreal. The third type of reading is also vital in connection to ideology as myth functions via distortion and ideology functions via illusion. Both are a kind of mirage with the *veiled* intention to deceive, to naturalize.

> "In order to gauge the political load of an object and the mythical hollow which espouses it, one must never look at things from the point of view of the signification,

39 {see Barthes, Barthes, pp. 104-106}

40 {see Barthes, Barthes, pp. 107-110, 112-113}

41 {see Barthes, Barthes, pp. 114-116}

> but from that of the signifier, of the thing which has been robbed; and within the signifier, from the point of view of the language-object, that is, of the meaning."[42]

Barthes explains the characteristic of myth is that it transforms meaning into form, which is always language robbery. Myth can develop its second-order schema from any meaning as well as the lack of meaning. The abstract concept of language itself implies that meaning can almost always be interpreted. Language offers myth an open-work meaning so that myth can insinuate itself into it which is a robbery by colonization. The best weapon against myth is to mythify in return, to produce an artificial myth.[43] Myth works through a *dis*placement of language that is marked by myth as a mode of domination. Myths as well as symbolism describe things as natural, which connects both to ideology. Thus to produce an artificial myth establishes a connection to ideology critique as well as to allegory. The works under discussion utilize the creation of artificial myths on an allegorical plane in order to reflect on *dis*tortion. "The oppressed is nothing and his language aims at transformation, it is poor. The oppressor is everything and his language aims at eternalizing, it is a rich multiform."[44] A language whose aim is eternalizing has to be considered as part of ideology, which is eternal. The reflection of the language of the oppressor is vital for a convincing ideology critique.

The last important aspect about myth for this argument is that myth is constituted of the loss of the historical quality of things. Barthes describes this procedure as *a conjuring trick* in which myth turns reality inside out. Myth empties reality of history and fills it with Nature. It removes from things their human meaning and thus the function of myth is to empty reality, to create a perceptible absence. In a bourgeois society the definition of myth is *de*politicized speech. Barthes focuses on the deeper meaning of political as a description of the whole of human relations in their real structure and that one must above all give an active value to the prefix *de-*. This prefix illustrates an operational movement and embodies a defaulting.[45] The metaphor of the *conjuring trick* brings us back to Priest and the metaphor of magic, which can serve as a substitution for art, ideology or mythology. The product of mythical magic is the *de*politicization of speech; myth liquidates history and *unveils* Nature. *De*politicization is another expression for *an atrophied sense of history,* which lies at the core of myth. The

42 {see Barthes, Barthes, p. 133}

43 {see Barthes, Barthes, pp. 118-120, 123}

44 {see Barthes, Barthes, p. 138}

45 {see Barthes, Barthes, p. 131}

prefix *de-* illustrates not only an operational movement but also indicates a profound *dis*enchantment with the world, which is encountered in all works within this discussion.

The network between allegory, ideology, and mythology now has to be tied to the body, as it is the center of attention. Foucault states the classical age discovered the body as object and target of power. The aim of docility is to join the analyzable (intelligible) body and the manipulable (useful) body. "A body is docile that may be subjected, used, transformed and improved." Foucault states that in every society the body was in the grip of power whose objective was control. The relation of docility-utility might be called disciplines, which became the general formulas of domination.[46] The three key words here are body, control and domination. The ruling class via ideology exerts control and domination. The objective is a docile and productive body. The transformation of the body is of importance here and will be closely observed. This argument traces the shift from the outside of the body to the inside of the body. Domination has to manipulate the outside as well as the inside in order to be effective. Foucault summarizes how discipline creates out of the bodies it controls an individuality that is endowed with four types of characteristics, which are cellular, organic, genetic, and combinatory. Discipline produces subjected, docile bodies and *increases the forces of the body in economic terms of utility* while discipline at the same time *diminishes the forces of the body in political terms of obedience*.[47] The four types of characteristics are traced in the works under discussion and analyzed. The product of discipline is a docile body and its mechanism itself is ambivalent as it *increases* and *diminishes* the forces of the body at the same time. Foucault suggests to describe the effects of power as production. Power produces reality, domains of objects, and rituals of truths.[48] The questions pursued are what kind of reality is produced and how are bodies affected by this production?

Foucault describes sexuality as an especially dense transfer point for relations of power and as the element in power relations with the greatest instrumentality. Foucault defines sexuality in this context as a historical construct, a network in which the stimulation of bodies, the intensification of pleasures, and the strengthening of controls as well as resistances are linked to one another in

46 {see Foucault, Discipline, pp. 136-137}

47 {see Foucault, Discipline, pp. 138, 167}

48 {see Foucault, Discipline, p. 194}

compliance with major strategies of knowledge and power.[49] Sexuality as a transfer point of power relations is one focal point of this argument. Modes of domination seek to employ sexuality in order to exert power first over the body and secondly over the mind. How is sexuality as a historical construct used in order to *control* and *manipulate* bodies?

Foucault outlines the deployment of sexuality operates according to mobile and contingent techniques of power. It engenders an extension of diverse forms of control and links a body that produces and consumes tightly to economy. The deployment of sexuality originates in creating, annexing, and penetrating bodies in order to increase control. Foucault concludes sexuality is a device of power and is linked to an intensification of the body, which is exploited as an object of knowledge and as an element in relations of power.[50] The link between bodies and economy is another focal point of this argument. How are bodies *annexed* and *penetrated*?

Foucault describes morality as a set of values individuals should observe. Those regulations are recommended through the intermediary of various agencies like the family, educational institutions, churches and others. Morality designates the conduct of an individual towards such regulations and illustrates the manner in which they obey or resist them. Foucault terms this level of phenomena the morality of behaviors.[51] The various agencies are what Althusser terms the Ideological State Apparatuses whose unity is secured by the ideology of the ruling class. These agencies aim at the reproduction of the relations of capitalist relations of exploitation.[52] As morality is recommended through the ISAs the conclusion is their aim is the reproduction of the relations of production. Morality is tightly knotted to the body that is at the center of attention. How is morality *obeyed* or *resisted*?

Foucault emphasizes "all moral action involves a relationship with the reality in which it is carried out, and a relationship with the self." Morality comprises two vital elements, which are *codes of behavior* and *forms of subjectivation*. In the case the *code* is emphasized he suggests to focus on the instances of authority that enforce the *code*. If an authority demands that a code must be observed and penalizes infractions then the subsequent subjectivation is based on a quasi-juridical form. The subject refers his conduct to a set of laws to which he must

49 {see Du Gay, Identity, pp. 102, 104

50 {see Du Gay, Identity, pp. 104-105}

51 {see Du Gay, Identity, p. 367}

52 {see Althusser, On Ideology, pp. 23, 28}

submit but there is always the risk of committing offenses that can make him liable to punishment. In the case the *forms of subjectivation* are emphasized the exact observance of codes may be relatively unimportant. The focus is laid on forms of relations with the self and on the practices that enable the subject to transform his own mode of being.[53] Morality incorporates an internal (forms of subjectivation) and an external relationship (codes of behavior). Both relationships need to be illuminated in order to establish an analysis of the mechanism of power. Both relationships are vital for the *de*substantialization of the subject and the production of a docile body. How important is the Cartesian split to power relations and total control?

According to Baudrillard, simulation of the third order is beyond equivalences and Manichean distinctions. Its aim is total control. "Thus, *lacking the real*, it is there that we must aim at order."[54] Allegory is the perfect literary device to aim at order as allegory itself is *lacking the real*. It exemplifies *de*referentialization because it is a system of differences. Mythology functions through *de*politicization and hence is founded on a reversal of reality. Ballard observes a reversal of the external world around us and the inner world of our minds. He positions reality on the inside of our minds and fiction on the outside, the world around us. "The writer's task is to invent reality."[55] The world around is has been turned into a world of signs and thus the artist must invent reality via the detour of a dark space. Power manipulates the outside as well as the inside of human bodies in order to achieve total control. Sometimes the codes of behavior are within special focus and sometimes the forms of subjectivation demand special attention. *De*substantianlization is the key within power relations, as transformation needs to be external as well as internal. Allegory makes mythology visible inside and outside of bodies and thus illuminates a double horizon. Baudrillard outlines strategic resistance is the refusal of meaning and of the spoken word. This strategy works through the doubling and returning of the systems own logic, it reflects meaning like a mirror and does not absorb it.[56] "It is useless to dream of revolution through content, useless to dream of a revelation through form, because the medium and the real are now in single nebula whose truth is indecipherable."[57] The artists within the range of this argument do not dream of

53 {see Du Gay, Identity, pp. 369-370}

54 {see Baudrillard, Simulation, pp. 21, 121}

55 {see Ballard, Crash, Preface}

56 {see Baudrillard, Simulation, pp. 85-86}

57 {see Baudrillard, Simulation, p. 83}

revolution through content as they work with substitution. They are *lacking a referent* and thus are themselves indecipherable. Their refusal of meaning becomes obvious in the enigmatic character of their works. Allegory as a natural mirror to ideologies is read as a strategic resistance to meaning and reflects the logic of the system.

The Last House on the Left (1972)

> Les Américains croient aux faits, mais pas à la facticité. Ils ne savent pas que le fait est factice, [...] c'est en ce sens que les Américains sont une véritable société utopique, dans leur religion du fait accompli, dans la naïveté de leur déductions, dans leur méconnaissance du malin génie des choses.[58]

Wes Craven's film *The Last House on the Left* (1972) opens the discussion about power relations. According to Robin Wood, the seventies are the Golden Age of American horror film. During the seventies the horror film genre became the most important of all American genres and perhaps the most progressive.[59] David A. Cook outlines *The Last House* is a reflexive indictment of the Americans high tolerance for violence. The film is about the rape and torture-murder of two young girls by a gang of criminals. Later they seek shelter in the home of one of their victim's parents but are identified by the parents who in their turn exact a horrific revenge.[60] *The Last House* does not only belong to the horror genre but also to pornography with regard to sexuality as well as violence. An article in *Variety* from 1970 began with the lead "If one word sums up trends in 1970 film exhibition in the U.S. it is 'pornography'"[61] Emanuel Barot describes the pornographic film as a sub-genre of the social-political film which subverts established hierarchies. It thematizes the *de*substantilization of traditional relations between the body, sex, standards and symbolic associations.[62] Thus Craven combines the progressive character of the horror genre with the subversive character of pornography. This combination is filmed with a particular technique that underlines their characteristic traits. Cook points out *The Last House* has a *cinéma verité* quality and a grim seriousness of purpose.[63] The film begins with the following statement: "The events you are about to witness are true. Names and locations have been changed to protect those individuals still living."

---

58 {see Baudrillard, Amérique, p. 84. "Americans believe in facts but not in artificiality. They do not know that facts are artificial [...] in this sense Americans are a truly utopian society which shows in their religion of accomplished facts, in the naivety of their reasoning, and in their misrecongition of the malicious character of things." [trans. mine]}

59 {see David A. Cook, Lost Illusions: American Cinema in the Shadow of Watergate and Vietnam, 1970 – 1979 (Berkeley 2002), pp. 220, 229}

60 {see Cook, Lost, p. 230}

61 {see Cook, Lost, p. 283}

62 {see Barot, Camera, p. 35}

63 {see Cook, Lost, p. 230}

Barthes outlines a work of art is at the very start mythified (made innocent) by its being fiction.[64] Craven uses a documentary opening statement and thus creates a strong counter-myth. *Its cinéma verité quality makes it guilty.* Stephen Silliman states a national malaise marked the seventies. Pride and optimism were replaced by guilt and self-doubt.[65] This guilt originates in the Americans high tolerance for violence. Writer and director Wes Craven states at the time of Vietnam there was a tremendous amount of very shocking footage. He was against the war and felt angry as well as repulsed by the violence from there. He observes there were sadistic and sexual overtones. American cinema did not show violence as it was shown in the footage. He points out there were no good guys and bad guys anymore. In order to achieve a *verité* sense of reality he employed basically a documentary crew. He was accused of having made the most un-American film ever. Craven outlines there are certain things one is not supposed to say or show and those mythologies were concocted to enforce this kind of *omission*. Producer Sean S. Cunningham was convinced the *cinéma verité quality* would make the film stronger and it wouldn't have to be this big overproduced numbing of the sensibilities.[66] Craven and Cunningham both felt violence was shown to audiences in a way that took away its repulsive nature and made it tolerable. Hence they deprived violence of its artificial character and created violence with sadistic and strong sexual overtones. The *cinéma verité* style is essential to this technique in order to counter the numbing. Méconnaissance is considered as a leitmotif of *The Last House* because the tolerance for violence is a direct result of *de*politicization. Mythology and morality are responsible for what can be addressed and the films tremendous *dis*regard for these recommendations shows audiences the dangerous extent of mèconnaisance. Althusser states ideology aims at the misrepresentation of the world to us.[67] *The cinéma verité style in The Last House has the task to politicize in order to expose relations of power behind ideology, mythology and morality.*

Omissions can only be established through the consent of the subjects of power relations. This consent is one abstract concept illustrated by *The Last House*. A Brechtian technique employed by the film is *de*psychologization. This

64 {see Barthes, Selected, p. 133}

65 {see Stephen Silliman, The "Old West" in the Middle East: U.S. Military Metaphors in Real and Imagined Indian Country , p.}

66 {see Wes Craven, The Last House on the Left (USA 1972), Documentary: Celluloid Crime of the Century}

67 {see Bertens, Literary, p. 84}

technique enables the focus on collective patterns of behavior rather than on the nuances of individual consciousness.[68] Barot outlines that political films thematize power, domination, and revolution. They depict relations between people, communities, individuals and the power of the state or interest groups. Their aim is to expose mechanisms of power relations and origins of revolutionary impulses as well as submissive behavior. "L'impératif démocratique" revolts against all kinds of tyranny and it is the main signification, which renders a film political or militant.[69] *The Last House* exposes power relations and traces the origins of submissive behavior, i.e. it is a political film. "L'impératif démocratique" finds expression in the progressive character of the horror genre, the subversive nature of pornography and the non-natural, constructed space of allegory. Barot emphasizes that a film may seem to be apolitical but in fact only plays the apolitical card in order to escape censorship.[70] Genre and allegory work as a protective agent against censorship because an open indictment of American politics in Vietnam and sadistic violence would have lead to censorship. *The Last House* may seem to be apolitical but after close examination the film is in fact very political.

Three aspects will be analyzed in order to expose power relations. The Collingwood family, the Krug family, and their children illustrate three different points in the constellation at work. "Mari and Junior are stuck in the rain" is a line from the last song of the film. Mari is the daughter of the Collingwoods and Junior is the son of Krug. Both are connected with each other through their relationship with pleasure. Krug makes Junior an addict and thus uses addiction as a means of direct control over his body. Junior's only pleasure is his next fix. Mari's idea of pleasure is to attend a concert by a band named 'Blood Lust' who *dis*members chicken on stage. Mari's sensibilities towards violence are strongly influenced by her idea of pleasure. In Junior's case pleasure directly numbs the body whereas Mari's senses are numbed. Both can be regarded as two parts of the same spectrum. They *are* the Cartesian split and illustrate how power relations have to influence body (Junior) and mind (Mari) on separate levels in order to achieve obedience. Jean-Francois Lyotard outlines pleasure is the enemy for the postmodernist thinker because it is judged to be the means by which the con-

68 {see Stam, Film, p. 147}

69 {see Emmanuel Barot, Camera Politica: Dialectique du Réalisme dans le Cinéma Politique et Militant (Groupes Medvedkine, Francesco Rosi, Peter Watkins) (Paris 2009), pp. 28-30, 36}

70 {see Barot, Camera, p. 35}

sumer is reconciled to the dominant ideology.[71] *The Last House* visualizes how Mari and Junior are reconciled to the dominant ideology via pleasure, which is a key task of relations of power. One important binary feature between counter cinema and mainstream cinema is “unpleasure vs pleasure.” Stam argues a danger within Brechtianism itself may be Puritanism that valorizes the working spectator as opposed to the enjoying spectator. For him, an effective film must offer a quantum of pleasure and Brechtian distantiation only works if there is a desire to be distanced.[72] The reality created by *The Last House* is continuously disturbing and aims at the working spectator who is not granted one passive moment. The film employs a *cinéma verité style* and edits antithetical scenes in order to cancel out pleasure. This strategy cannot be designated as 'puritanical attitude towards filmic pleasure' as pleasure itself is indicted in the film as an origin of alienation. Is there really the option to 'desire to be distanced?' The premise of the film is that people *are* distanced and that this not a natural condition but a non-natural condition which is misrecognized.

Barot states the political film aims at crystallization and analysis of contradictions, which animate *social relations* and how people experience those relations. The political film conveys an interpretation of the meaning of struggle and moreover proposes a *visualization* of what a struggle is as well as the conditions it requires.[73] The focus of Brechtian film criticism is laid on politics and in particular on certain goals of aesthetics in films. The goal of importance here is the V-effect (Verfremdungseffekt), which *de*conditions the audience and renders strange the lived social world. The effect aims at freeing socially conditioned phenomena from the stamp of familiarity and to reveal them as other than natural.[74] The working aesthetic of *The Last House* is a *cinéma verité* quality that incessantly *de*conditions the audience. Sexual molestation, rape, torture and *dis*memberment become extremely 'verfremdet' and thus render the lived social world strange. As Craven felt the presentation of violence was artificial he rendered it real via the films *cinéma verité* style.

The two violent parties of the film are the two families and their violence may have different origins but both are cruel and merciless. The lack of motivation on the part of Krug and company is so apparent that it is defined as *de*psychologization. Carla Freccero suggests the serial killer serves the function of a

71 {see Gelder, The Horror, p. 287-288}

72 {see Stam, Film, pp. 148-150}

73 {see Barot, Camera, pp. 12-13}

74 {see Stam, Film, pp. 146-147}

fetish in public culture. He is the means of the disavowal of institutionalized violence and the seriality of his violent acts marks the place of recognition in this disavowal. Through the serial killer public culture recognizes and simultaneously refuses the violence-saturated quality of culture, which situates the source in an individual with a psycho-sexual dysfunction. Thus violence can be located in an individuals dysfunction rather than in the social order.[75] Craven states he was repulsed by the violence perpetrated during the Vietnam War, which is institutionalized violence. Krug and company are individuals with psycho-sexual dysfunctions and represent the abstract concept of institutionalized violence that originates in the social order. Freccero concludes what is somatized in the figure of the serial killer is an ideology of violence that represents violence as something originating in the private sphere. The popularity of the vehicle of the serial killer as a sign of social disease may be read as an indication. It illustrates the degree to which history is already successfully censored. History's violence and the violence of the state are embodied in the serial killer.[76] *The Last House* as allegory does not represent violence as originating in the private sphere. As it is impossible to keep an abstract concept abstract it has to be visualized. The film is a surreal interpretation of events as censored history is full of *omissions* and *lacunes*. Krug and company discuss what kind of crime could never be forgiven and come to the conclusion it is a sex crime. They ask themselves what crime might qualify as the sex crime of the century.[77] Sex and crime combined are essential here as they refer to abject violence. Julia Kristeva outlines the abject is situated on the edges of primal repression, which discovers a corporeal and signifying symptom and sign: repugnance, disgust and abjection. Object and sign tumble over into the impossible real and appear as abjection.[78] Cunningham terms the energy of the film as raw and Craven states the film is not dated due to its primal quality.[79] The films raw and primal quality originates in the approach of primal repression. Craven was especially disgusted by the violence of the war in Vietnam, as it was a violence of the State. Sex crime is read as a *substitution* for war crime, which is an example par excellence for what cannot be represented as history has censored it. It is founded on a *lack of reality* and an *atrophied*

75 {see Carla Freccero, Historical Violence, Censorship, and the Serial Killer: The Case of American Psycho, p. 48}

76 {see Freccero, Historical Violence, pp. 48-49}

77 {see Craven, The Last House on the Left}

78 {see Julia Kristeva, Powers of Horror (New York 1982), p. 11}

79 {see Craven, The Last House on the Left}

sense of history. Barthes states in passing from history to Nature, myth acts economically. Myth abolishes the complexity of human acts and gives them the simplicity of essence. It organizes a world that has no depth and subsequently is without contradictions. It establishes a blissful clarity in which things appear to mean something by themselves. Myth makes things innocent and gives them a natural justification not by rendering an explanation but by way of making a statement of fact.[80] *The Last House* as a counter-myth aims at making things guilty and its allegorical cadre renders its non-natural quality visible. The missing depth of the world is expressed in the misrecognition of the 'malin génie des choses.' The dinner sequence in the black room exemplifies this line of argument. It is the only scene without a conventional setting and thus unique. It can be concluded that what is illustrated in this scene is essential for the film.

Figure 1: The Last House on the Left © Abstract enactment between two opposing relations of subjugation

The black room is an ideological space, an actual pure illusion. The room exemplifies the American belief in facts and the utterly naïve reasoning of Americans.[81] According to Marx, the mind and consciousness of the petit-bourgeois class do not extend beyond the limits which this class has set to its

80 {see Barthes, Barthes, p. 132}

81 {see Baudrillard, Amérique, p. 84}

activities[82] This limitation is part of *Identification*, a principal figure of what Barthes terms pseudo-physis. The Other is denied, ignored or transformed into himself by the petit-bourgeois.[83] The behavior as well as the clothing of Krug and company reveals a discrepancy but the Collingwoods are conditioned to misrecognize the evil character of things.

Craven employs a particular language when he refers to the Collingwoods. On the occasion of Mari Collingwood's birthday the parents toast to their *'princess.'* Dr. Collingwood toasts to his wife and terms her the *'queen.'* Sadie's commentary on the house of the family is that it makes her wish she were a *'lady.'* Krug calls them with contempt 'goddamn *high-class* tight-ass freakos.' The last song in the film refers to the house of the family as 'Collingwood *Manor*.' It is concluded Craven names them bourgeois and thus counter-acts bourgeois ex-nomination, which characterizes bourgeois ideology as well as myth.[84] The sensibilities of the Collingwoods are numbed, frozen and thus passive. In the beginning of the film Dr. Collingwood's comment on the news is that in the outside world its just murder and mayhem. He then asks his wife what she cooks for dinner. The rhetorical figure at work here is inoculation. The collective imagination is immunized by means of a small inoculation of acknowledged evil.[85] The media as part of the ISAs are responsible for this inoculation. Krug and company are introduced to the audience by the radio. Craven works here on two levels as he demonstrates the effect of the media on the protagonists and then transfers the effect on the audience. He thus reveals a mythology of violence that takes away the history of violence and naturalizes it.

Barthes states man in a bourgeois society is at every turn plunged into a false Nature. The mythologist attempts to find again under the assumed innocence of the most unsophisticated relationships the profound alienation, which this innocence is meant to make one accept.[86] This assumed innocence is symbolized by the peace symbol. Mari's birthday present is a necklace with a peace symbol and the symbol is on a poster in her room. A symbol is connected to ideology but it is also a form of *de*politicized speech. The peace symbol is a means to make one accept the profound alienation that results from power relations. The frame exemplifies this abstract concept, as the peace symbol is essen-

---

82 {see Barthes, Barthes, p. 141}

83 {see Barthes, Barthes, pp. 140-141 }

84 {see Barthes, Barthes, p. 135}

85 {see Barthes, Barthes, p. 140}

86 {see Barthes, Barthes, p. 146}

tial for tolerating institutionalized violence that is embodied by Krug and company. During the course of the film the peace symbol unveils their sex crime and thus is reversed into politicized speech. The allegorical image also signifies a lack of representation and thus questions representation itself.

Figure 2: The Last House on the Left © The frame illustrates the gulf between the real (institutionalized violence) and the ideal (peace)

One goal of Brecht's aesthetics in film is to involve the spectator in the process of constructing meaning, as there is an immanence of meaning amongst contradictory voices.[87] But it has to be considered that another leitmotif of postmodernism is *dis*sensus rather than consensus.[88] Foucault states *relations of subjugation* should operate in their multiplicity, their differences, their specificity as well as their reversibility. They must be studied as *relations of force* that intersect, refer to one another or come into conflict and strive to negate one another.[89] Craven created an *allegory of relations of subjugation* that come into conflict with each other and ultimately destroy each other. If they are *unveiled* as what they really are and as such recognized they must negate each other. *Dissensus* is the only viable option for Craven who involves the spectator in the

87 {see Stam, Film, p. 146}

88 {see Stam, Film, p. 301}

89 {see Foucault, Society, p. 266}

construction of meaning but as the film is founded on a lack of reality (*omitted* history) meaning is absent.

Two points shall be mentioned here and they are the point of transition to the next chapter. In the beginning of the film Sadie calls Krug a male chauvinist pig. In the end Krug tells Dr. Collingwood: "*We* are just playing games, Doc." These two points both concern Krug and will be elaborated in the context of *Punishment Park*.

Punishment Park (1970)

> Mahagonny – does not exist. Mahagonny – is not a location. Mahagonny – is just an invented locution.[90]

The British auteur Peter Watkins created with his film *Punishment Park* a unique vision of America and no discussion about *relations of power* can be possible without *Punishment Park.* Barot describes in his essay *Camera Politica* the work of Watkins as emblematic in his choice of intransigent subversion. *Punishment Park* illustrates the mechanism of martial law according to the McCarran Act. People are condemned because they subvert moral and political security. The condemned can choose between a long sentence of imprisonment and Punishment Park where they can be free after a few days if they reach a certain point without getting arrested by the guards. The game theme of the park is defined by the hunt (game) on people. The condemned are not portrayed as heroes as their fight for survival renders the whole spectrum of human experience visible form self-mastery to the release of the basest instincts. The documentary effect of the hearings and the interviews cause the audience to believe they watch a reportage. Peter Watkins's commentary on that effect is rather poignant. He asks how can a film be perceived as real regardless of how 'real' the documentary cadre may ever be if the place itself ('Punishment Park' in America) does not exist?[91] This statement illustrates that there is no referent and thus there is no equivalence between the sign and the real. *Punishment Park* is founded on the principle of difference in order to express what cannot be expressed.

> Le principe allégorique, ici, tourne à plein. Par cette dimension intrinsèquement non représentative, dystopique, *Punishment Park* allégorise le réel lui-même, le met profondément en question, puisqu'il montre que le possible en est constitutif.[92]

Punishment Park is as non-existent as America because both are abstract ideas. This argument pursues the line that *Punishment Park* creates a counter-myth on an allegorical plane. It is an abstract idea about relations of power in America during the early seventies and shows that the possible is an essential part of the real. It reveals how the mechanism of myth works whose maxim is: "More real

---

90 {see Bertolt Brecht, Rise and Fall of the City of Mahagonny (London 2007), p. vii}

91 {see Barot, Camera, pp. 88, 100}

92 {see Barot, Camera, p. 100. "The allegorical principle operates here in its full spectrum. The dystopic and inherently non-representative dimension in Punishment Park allegorizes the real itself. The film profoundly questions reality because it shows that the possible is constituent." [trans. mine]}

than the real, that is how the real is abolished."[93] Mahagonny as well as Punishment Park are both invented locutions and the very term Punishment Park is of great importance for an analysis because the term itself is a *dis*location of language and it is non-natural. The term has the ability to mirror ideology, which describes things as natural because it is founded on a lack of reality but is perceived as real. One important binary feature between counter cinema and mainstream cinema is reality vs fiction.[94] Watkins invents a complex reality because he is aware that the world is pure fiction. *Punishment Park* as counter myth (counter cinema) creates reality. Myth is experienced as innocent speech because its intentions are naturalized. The myth consumer takes the signification for a system of facts whereas any semiological system is a *system of values*.[95] A look at the terms separately will illuminate how a *system of values* functions. Punishment refers to the act of punishment and is derived from the Latin word poena, which means penalty or pain. Park is defined as a piece of ground in or near a city kept as a place of beauty and recreation. It is also an arena or stadium used especially for ball games.[96] The term Park refers to a non-violent place and to a game that follows certain rules. It is argued the term Park naturalizes the intentions of the term Punishment. All the condemned prefer Punishment Park to imprisonment and the reason is on the one hand the long sentences of their imprisonment as opposed to three days in Punishment Park. But on the other hand they all believe it is innocent speech. Signification is turned into an 'empty parasitical form' as the actual meaning of the term Punishment Park is alienated. What needs to be expressed cannot be expressed and a detour is used. According to Baudrillard, '(le sens est né de l'érosion des mots, les significations sont nées des l'érosion des signes).'[97] The conclusion is this erosion at the source is illustrated via the marriage between the terms Punishment and Park. Thus the term Punishment Park exemplifies the split between language and world.

Punishment Park is a violent place and the anarchy of power abolishes all rules. For Baudrillard, Disneyland is the epitome of all the entangled orders of simulacra. His ideological analysis of Disneyland describes it as a digest of the American way of life, a praise of *American values,* and an idealization of a con-

93 {see Baudrillard, Simulation, p. 81}

94 {see Stam, Film, p. 148}

95 {see Barthes, Barthes, p. 118}

96 {see Webster's New Encyclopedic Dictionary, pp. 730, 821}

97 {see Baudrillard, Amérique, p. 9. "(meaning is born out of the erosion of words, signification is born out of the erosion of signs)" [trans. mine]}

tradictory reality. This is a process of masking that Disneyland is a simulation of the third order. Disneyland is a deterrence machine.[98] Punishment Park is also a deterrence machine. Punishment Park is described by an off-voice as a necessary training for law officers and the national guard of the country in the *control* of those elements who seek the violent overthrow of the US government and the means of providing a *punitive deterrent* for said subversive elements.[99] The game park theme serves as a simulation and reveals an *American system of values.*

> « Il se peut que la vérité de l'Amérique ne puisse apparaître qu'à un Européen, puisque lui seul trouve ici le simulacre parfait, celui de l'immanence et de la transcription matérielle de toutes les valeurs. Les Américains, eux, n'ont aucun sens de la simulation. »[100]

Baudrillard's statement holds also true for Watkins, as his approach is completely different from Cravens. Watkins film may at first seem more direct than Cravens film but it is also far more complex. Both are founded on a lack of reality but Watkins adds a political context whereas Craven's political context is obscured. Craven plays the apolitical card in order to escape censorship and Watkins embraces the consequences of playing the political card. Perhaps only a European like Watkins can approach simulation in this manner. Both films have a *cinéma vérité* quality but Craven focuses more on the sensual whereas Watkins aims more at the cerebral. In order to address the sensual Craven employs sexuality as a transfer point for relations of power. Watkins focuses on the cerebral and thus employs the morality of behaviors in order to show obedience as well as resistance. Barot outlines the impossibility to approach political cinema without having an idea about social or political struggles. He emphasizes the importance to pay attention to the aspired exploitation and oppression within the struggle and to the nature of history itself.[101] *Punishment Park* addresses class issues, gender issues, racial issues, war issues, civil issues, social issues but within the range of this argument focus is laid on civil issues. Kent State is a landmark with regard to civil rights in America in 1970. Cook emphasizes the

98 {see Baudrillard, Simulacra, p.12}

99 {see Watkins, Punishment Park}

100 {see Baudrillard, Amérique, p. 32. "It may be that the truth about America is only accessible to Europeans. Only Europeans discover in America the perfect simulacrum which is inherent and transcribes all values into things. Americans themselves have not the slightest sense for simulation." [trans mine] }

101 {see Barot, Camera, p. 12}

most extreme expression of a paranoid sense of imminent extinction that Kent State had fostered among Americas youth was Peter Watkins's independently produced *Punishment Park*. Unfortunately the film received limited distribution due to its highly controversial potential.[102] A look at the historical facts is important for a more comprehensive understanding of the film. On May 1, 1970, two or three thousand students from Kent State University surged through the town of Kent. They broke shop windows and battled with the police. The following night a fire was set at the school's old wooden ROTC building. These incidents were enough reason for Governor James A. Rhodes to call in troops of the 145th Infantry from the Ohio National Guard. He stated their mission was to eradicate the communist element and compared the Kent students to Hitler Youth. On May 4, about two thousand students gathered on the campus of Kent State University and thousands more gathered at a distance. Soldiers tried to break up the crowd of demonstrators with fear gas and ultimately they fired at the demonstrators. Four students were dead and eleven wounded. Richard Nixon voiced his opinion of antiwar kids before Kent State and described them as bums who blew up campuses. Students on college should be grateful and not "storming around about this *issue.*" A father of one of the dead students countered this statement with the following words: "My child was not a bum." After the shock of the killings at Kent State faded the students themselves had to face a country that did not like their 'ingratitude' or their 'arrogance.' Their battle cry "Fuck Richard Nixon!" did not either win the parents over who paid tuition neither those who could not afford it.[103] On October 16, a state grand jury indicted twenty-five students and university officials with regard to the riots at Kent State in May. The jurors found the National Guardsmen could not be held liable because they fired into the crowd. They were *justified,* as they believed their lives were in danger. In the last days of 1970, the press reflected on Richard Nixon and Walter Cronkite asked correspondents what they regarded as the most important event of the year. John Lawrence answered Kent State as it had shown Middle America that the *penalty for protest could be death.*[104] In *Punishment Park* the defendant Nancy Jane Smith refers directly to Kent state and the ensuing paranoia she experienced as a student.[105] Hunter S. Thompson describes

102 {see Cook, Lost, p. 174}

103 {see Richard Reeves, President Nixon: Alone in the White House (2001), pp. 212-213, 209, 225}

104 {see Reeves, President, pp. 269, 291}

105 {see Watkins, Punishment Park}

Richard Nixon as a cheap crook and a war criminal who connived to have protesting students attack and slain by troops from the National Guard.[106] Kent State as a symbol for *'penalty for protest can be death'* is one central aspect of ideology critique in *Punishment Park*. Lawrence's reflection on 1970 is literally translated by Watkins in *Punishment Park*. The killings at Kent State also divided the country and Watkins perceived the strategy of the government. The defense counsel in the film states it is quite clear to him that instead of trying to bring estranged and excluded Americans such as the defendants back into the national community the administration has chosen to accept and exploit the present division within the country and to side with what it considers as the majority. Instead of the politics of reconciliation it has chosen *politics of polarization*.[107] In *Punishment Park* the defendant Jay Kaufman asks the tribunal if they do know the difference between a patriot and a chauvinist? He outlines that chauvinism describes an absurd loyalty. Later Alison Michener states she is not loyal to the government because it is against the people.[108] It is concluded *loyalty* is a crucial issue and a government, which penalizes civil and social crimes with death, does not deserve loyalty as it is against the people. The strategy of the government exemplifies how basic freedoms are *dis*mantled and national issues are exploited for political advantage. Another analogy with *The Last House* becomes apparent as Krug was described as male chauvinist pig. Krug as a representative of institutionalized violence is read in this context as a person with an absurd loyalty towards a government that is against the people. Ultimately, he himself is against the people like the representatives of repressive state violence in *Punishment Park*.

Barot describes Watkins subversive use of allegory as a method to distinguish *what* is shown and *how* it is shown. Allegory is an expression of the attempt to unsettle the concepts of the real and politics.[109] Here Barot alludes to auteurism and how attention shifted from the "what" to the "how." Auteurism thus reveals that style itself has personal, ideological and even metaphysical reverberations.[110] The structure of *Punishment Park* is open-ended as we follow Corrective Group 638 through their trial and we follow Corrective Group 637

106 {see Hunter S. Thompson, Better Than Sex: Confessions of a Political Junkie (New York 1995), p. 243}

107 {see Watkins, Punishment Park}

108 {see Watkins, Punishment Park}

109 {see Barot, Camera, p. 93}

110 {see Stam, Film, pp. 89, 92}

through Punishment Park. The film ends with Corrective Group 638 on its way to Punishment Park and thus the end is also the beginning. The open-end of the film reflects an endless cycle and has ideological implications. According to Barot, in order to make a film about politics the film itself has to be *politicized*. The *form (how)* of the film itself and the *content (what)* are inextricably linked with each other. For Barot, the central concept of *allegory* serves as an 'anchorage point.' Watkins transforms film into an instrument within a political struggle. Film itself with its contents and its construction modes as well as production modes becomes the very principle it is supposed to embody. Barot defines Watkins's leitmotif as the resistance to different repressive aspects of dominant film making itself, which he calls *Monoform*. This *Monoform* includes montage and the structural narrative employed by commercial television and cinema.[111] The narrative structure (e.g. montage, multiple diegesis) of *Punishment Park* is not only a rejection of dominant filmmaking but also has metaphysical reverberations. Allegory as an anchorage point is perceived as the trademark of an auteur and finds expression in the *content* as well as in the *form* of *Punishment Park*.

> You talk like as if this is some great civilized, non-violent place. And it ain't. America is as psychotic as it is powerful and violence is the only goddamn thing that will command your attention. […] This country, this America, was born in violence. Now revolution is a violent thing.[112]

Barot emphasizes the most obvious in the work of Watkins is that the struggle against alienation cannot be fought with the *means of alienation*.[113] Foucault states discipline fixes as it arrests movements, it clears up confusion, and it *dissipates* compact groupings of individuals wandering about the country in unpredictable ways. Discipline must neutralize the effects of counter-power as agitations, revolts, or spontaneous organizations may establish horizontal conjunctions.[114] In *Punishment Park* discipline functions via violence and counter-violence is used to create more antagonism towards those who use it. The *means of alienation* are not a viable option in the struggle against repression. The *form* and the *content* of the film both illustrate the rejection of the *means of alienation*. This is an important analogy with *The Last House* as the Collingwood's embrace of violence portrays the cataclysmic effects of the use of the *means of alienation* against alienation. Craven's montage technique and *cinéma vérité*

111 {see Barot, Camera, pp. 23-25, 89}

112 {see Watkins, Punishment Park}

113 {see Barot, Camera, p. 93}

114 {see Foucault, Discipline, p. 219}

style are also a rejection of commercial cinema. It is concluded an efficient rejection of the *means of alienation* must include *form* as well as *content*.

Barthes states revolution utilizes a speech that is initially and finally political, which excludes myth. The left defines itself in relation to the oppressed and the speech of the oppressed can only be poor, monotonous and immediate.[115] The following quote from the film illustrates the speech of the oppressed and its monotonous quality. The quote also illustrates the whole spectrum of an immoral dimension in America.

> I am not immoral. You want me to tell you what is immoral? War is immoral. Poverty is immoral. Racism is immoral. Police brutality is immoral. Oppression is immoral. Genocide is immoral. Imperialism is immoral. This country represents all those things.[116]

Watkins creates a strong counter-myth because of his employment of the powerful speech of the oppressor and he manages to incorporate a fractured and contradictory multitude of voices and points of views. He creates a complex network structure in order to make *relations of subjugation* visible. "It's like this whole fucking game is like a revolution and we are in it. And we have got to either win or die."[117] This quote shows how game and revolution are interwoven with each other. But there is still the *méconnaissance* of a mere possibility of winning the game. "They believe in protest and ritual defiance and yet they are willing to participate fully in the rules established by the police for these games expecting that they will come out all right if they make the flag."[118] They are blinded by their *méconnaissance* of the evil character of things. Baudrillard outlines that neither the desert nor the game are free spaces. They are finite spaces with a center that is the soul of the game or the heart of the desert.[119] It is argued at the center is immorality.

> Le désert est partout et sauve l'insignifiance. [...] Ici, dans la société la plus morale qui soit, l'espace est vraiment immoral. Ici, dans la société la plus conforme qui soit, les dimensions sont immorales. C'est cette immoralité qui rend la distance légère et le voyage *infini*, c'est elle qui purifie les muscles de leur fatigue.[120]

---

115 {see Barthes, Barthes, p. 135, 137}

116 {see Watkins, Punishment Park}

117 {see Watkins, Punishment Park}

118 {see Watkins, Punishment Park}

119 {see Jean Baudrillard, Amérique (Paris 1986), p. 123}

120 {see Baudrillard, Amérique, pp. 13-14. [italics mine] "The desert is everywhere and its insignificance remains unaffected. [...] Within the most moral society is a truly immoral space. Within the most conform society the dimensions are immoral. This immorality

Watkins combines the metaphor of the game and the metaphor of the desert in order to develop an allegory whose central issue is to visualize an unfree space created by the ISAs and RSAs. Althusser emphasizes the State and its Apparatuses only have meaning from the point of view of the class struggle as they ensure *class oppression* and guarantee the conditions of exploitation as well as its reproduction. *There is no class struggle without antagonistic classes.* Class struggle of the ruling class is directly related to resistance, revolt and class struggle of the ruled class.[121] The game is a metaphor for class struggle (revolution) and the dominance of the ruling class. Krug also plays games with Dr. Collingwood and thus he is situated right in the middle of class struggle and exploitation.

According to Barot, Watkins thematizes in his oeuvre on a grand scale the *illusion of liberty* which surfaces with the *emergence of power.* His films show the mechanism of reactionary powers, exploitation and oppression. They choose the moment when power is swayed by revolution but in the end power triumphs.[122] The relations of power (the rules of the game) are established by the ruling class and can be changed at any point. *The assumption this game can be won is a deception, as it is not designed to be won.* "The whole country is lawless, violent, explosive, demoniacal. It's in the air, in the climate, in the ultra-grandiose landscape, [...] the opposition of laws and languages, the contradictoriness of temperaments, principles, needs, requirements."[123] The 'ultra-grandiose landscape' described by Henry Miller is itself the expression of an inherent contradiction. Watkins illustrates with the desert an endless space and a finite space at the same time. Watkins and Miller both believe in a lawless America whose very nature is violent. The following frame shows two important points. On the one hand the 'ultra-grandiose landscape' underlines the immoral dimension of oppressive power relations. On the other hand the frame corresponds to one basic assumption of this argument. Barot points out how Watkins establishes a homology between the duality of facts and meaning and the *duality of the individual and the universal.* He concludes a realist has to access a totality, which permits him to bring to surface the universal individual. *Thus he creates a ge-*

---

renders the distance short and the voyage infinite. This immorality purifies the muscles from their exhaustion." [trans. mine]}

121 {see Althusser, On Ideology, p. 58}

122 {see Barot, Camera, p. 101}

123 {see Miller, The Obelisk, p. 170}

neric figure that embodies the typical duality of an individual character and historical circumstances.[124]

Figure 3: Punishment Park © The desert as an expression of a violent and an immoral country

The frame is so powerful as it shows the generic figures dual character. Miller and Watkins share the same vision of America, which is reflected in the 'ultra-grandiose landscape' and thus is a timeless vision.

> The only legitimate thing that I can think of doing is to use my body or well-being or freedom or life as to back up what I say. At another time, the honorable thing or the right thing to do might be to be a policeman or to be President. Right now I think the honorable thing to do is to be a criminal.[125]

A detainee at Punishment Park states his work is not committed to the revolution but it is a *commitment to sanity*. These statements are the point of transition to the next chapter and represent its nexus. Focuses are laid on the *dis*solution of Manichean distinctions and on the necessity of a commitment to sanity.

124 {see Barot, Camera, pp. 18, 19, 21, 23}

125 {see Watkins, Punishment Park}

The Room (1971)

> It is so hard to have any *hope* about anything, after you see how completely *inhuman* people are.[126]

Henry Miller outlines in order to be accepted you must nullify yourself. It is important to be indistinguishable from the herd. Even dreams have to be alike or otherwise you are not an American.[127] Norman Mailer meditates in an essay on Henry Miller about the fact that Miller does not become more compatible with time. Miller is almost treated as if he wasn't an American author and Mailer emphasizes nobody could be more American than Henry Miller. He concludes that Miller has not lost his *enigmatic* aura and his work is too complex and perhaps too out of measure.[128] The creation of too complex work distinguishes one from the herd and leads to being regarded as an un-American artist. James Richard Giles discusses in *Understanding Hubert Selby, Jr.* the seeming foreignness of *The Room* and the Americanness of Selby as a writer because structure and tone of the novel are more reminiscent of European writers.[129] Selby is as enigmatic as Miller and both are committed to non-conformity. Foucault states the whole domain of the non-conforming is punishable.[130] The 'punishment' is being regarded as un-American and being excluded from the American literary tradition. The irony is that nobody could be more American than Selby or Miller. Giles points out that it is not his subject matter that defines Selby as a profoundly revolutionary American writer but his intuitive understanding of *the nature of power in American society* and his determination to give voice to the powerless.[131] The central question is how is *the nature of power in American society* portrayed in *The Room?*

Within the range of this argument Selby is perceived not as the 'poet of male violence'[132] but as the *poet of terror*. Tambling states emotional states like Anger, Envy, Fear or Revenge can be considered as personifications and thus are allegorical. The two passions Pity and Terror belong to tragedy.[133] “And as he

---

126 {see Watkins, Punishment Park. [italics mine]}

127 {see Miller, The Obelisk, p. 178}

128 {see Ronald Gottesman, Critical Essays on Henry Miller (New York 1992), p. 239}

129 {see James Richard Giles, Understanding Hubert Selby, Jr. (Columbia 1998), pp. 50}

130 {see Foucault, Discipline, pp. 178-179}

131 {see Giles, Understanding, p. 11 }

132 {see Giles, Understanding, p. 54}

133 {see Tambling, Allegory, pp. 7, 10-11 }

looked at the beautiful expression of terror on their faces he could feel the tension of their bodies.[...] The most exciting beauty he had ever viewed."[134] This quote illustrates the way Selby meditates on terror as well as humanity in a Blakean sense. He makes a connection between terror and the human form divine. Giles outlines *The Room* largely abandons any concept of fictional plot and merges 'reality' with the psychotic fantasies of its protagonist who is an unnamed man jailed for a reason that Selby never explains. For Giles, this anonymous prisoner exemplifies the forgotten and powerless contemporary American urban male.[135] *The Last House* as well as *The Room* orbit around a sex crime and sadistic, authoritative violence. The internal reality of the protagonist is illuminated in order to illustrate his relations with the external fiction around him. *The Room*'s disturbing narrative gained it the best reviews of any Selby novel and he himself comments on the novel in the following way: "*The Room* was the most disturbing book I have ever read. I mean, it is really a disturbing book, Jesus Christ! I didn't read it for twelve years after I wrote it."[136] This argument pursues the idea that Selby does not give voice to the powerless but that he voices different shades of powerlessness, which are universal. This would explain the disturbing effect the book had on him. Selby outlines that the basis for *The Room* can be perceived like variations on a musical theme, like an *enigma variation*. There is the theme of a prisoner's reality and variations like his memories and his projections. For Selby the novel is as American as his other novels but more in an implicit way, in its *undertones*.[137] Henry Miller is convinced music is the manifestation of action without activity. It is "the noiseless sound made by the swimmer in the ocean of consciousness."[138] Tambling points out that music may be regarded as writing, which is allegoric in structure but on a metonymic level.[139] The nature of allegorical writing is elusive and it's meaning often indeterminate. An important key term in allegorical interpretation is *enigma*.[140] Miller and Selby are enigmatic authors whose works are voyages into the self. A connection arises between enigma variations, text as music, and an allegorical reading. *The Room* is the strongest agent of a liquidation of all referentials so far in

134 {see Hubert Selby, Jr., The Room (London 2011), p. 77}
135 {see Giles, Understanding, p. 3}
136 {see Giles, Understanding, pp. 3-4}
137 {see Giles, Understanding, pp. 49, 52}
138 {see Miller, The Obelisk, p. 322}
139 {see Tambling, Allegory, p. 161}
140 {see Copeland, Cambridge, p. 2}

this argument. Whereas Watkins plays with the illusion of reality and Craven inserts abstract spaces Selby's inclination is towards complete abstractedness.

For Lukács, the creation of *typical* characters can successfully produce a fictional world that is a reflection of life with all its motivating contradictions.[141] He further argues the human significance, the specific individuality of these *typical* characters, cannot be separated from the context in which they were created.[142] *The Room* was published in 1971 and this argument pursues the line that the historical context is of immense importance. Craven was appalled by sadistic violence in Vietnam, which is the nexus of his film. Selby focuses in *The Room* on police brutality, crime, punishment, rape and retribution, which forms a quite similar nexus as *The Last House*. One of the most important events of 1970 for Dan Rather was the Calley trial. For him it symbolized what made up America in 1970. It stood for mixed emotions, confusion and complexities over *'where we're going, who we are, what is our leadership.'*[143] Joseph Goldstein, Burke Marshall, and Jack Schwartz address in *The Limits of Law: On Establishing Civilian Responsibility for the Enforcement of Laws Against War Crimes* the investigation of war crimes in My Lai and the cover-up. On March 29, 1969, civilian and veteran of Vietnam Ronald L. Ridenhour wrote a letter to the Secretary of Defense and others that stated 'something very black' had occurred in Vietnam. He had heard persistent rumors of massacres at My Lai and his personal decision to go public prompted action.[144] Ridenhour's letter emphasizes the importance of *equality* of every man before the law, which is a central point in *The Room*.

> Exactly what did, in fact, occur in the village of "Pinkville" in March, 1968 I do not know for certain, but I am convinced that it was something very black indeed. I remain irrevocably persuaded that if you and I do truly believe in the principles, of justice and the *equality* of every man, however humble, before the law, that form the very backbone that this country is founded on, then we must press forward a widespread and public investigation of this matter with all our combined efforts. I think it was Winston Churchhill who once said: "A country without a conscience is a country without a soul, and a country without a soul is a country that cannot survive."[145]

141 {see Abrams, A Glossary, p. 243}

142 {see Bertens, Literary, p. 91}

143 {see Reeves, President, p. 291. [italics mine]}

144 {see William Peers, The My Lai Massacre and its Cover-Up: Beyond the Reach of Law? (New York 1976), pp. 1, 10, 33}

145 {see Peers, The My Lai, p. 37}

The crimes against the inhabitants of My Lai included individual and group acts of murder, rape, sodomy, maiming, assault on non-combatants, the mistreatment and killing of detainees. Secretary of the Army Howard H. Callaway described it as *'incident'* which is a fraudulent word play and a form of institutional denial by which persons in authority absolve themselves of responsibility. Judge Irving Younger observed: "The first task of free men is to call things by their name." As of November 1974, Lt. Calley was the only person among the 30 held to account through the system of military justice. The term 'justified for military reasons' was the *mask* for lawlessness and self-deception in the Americal Division after My Lai. The magnitude of crimes at My Lai might have been exceptional but they were neither unique nor isolated. The overall goal of military training is *the molding of reflexively obedient killers.* The question is whether or how the training in the law of war can give authoritative voice to the obligation to *diso*-bey criminal orders with regard to this goal. Self-correcting mechanisms do not work under stress and as the subsequent Watergate affair shows they should not be relied on in matters of great public importance. The Peers report reveals the military's institutional incapacity to deter, or punish, or even bring to light that kind of crime. Institutional changes are required in order to make the nation's commitment to the Nuremberg principle credible. An appropriate body like a congressional committee has to explore how best to separate from the military responsibility the function of investigating and prosecuting crimes and related obstructions of justice. "*The law does not fail when crimes are committed, for no law against crime – not even against murder – can prevent all crimes. The law fails when it does not seek to discover and hold responsible those who commit crime.*"[146]

The following quote is from a reverie in which the protagonist addresses a special investigating committee of the United States Senate: "... if we unfurl and hold high the banner of truth so injustice will be exposed whenever it exists, whether it be in the largest of cities or smallest of hamlets; in the brightest of spaces or the darkest of corners." The chairman of the committee agrees with the protagonist and underlines that the country can be made truly free only in defending the truth, by seeking out the guilty and by exposing lies.[147] One focal point of the novel is that the law cannot prevent crime but it has the obligation to expose crime and to hold those responsible who commit crime. Selby's use of a 'special investigating committee' indicates his *dis*trust in the states responsibility

146 {see Peers, The My Lai, pp. 1-3, 6-8, 11, 14 [italics mine]}

147 {see Selby, The Room, pp. 111, 112, 116}

to investigate crimes. Unfortunately, the Calley trial exemplifies the failure of the law and Selby anticipated that.

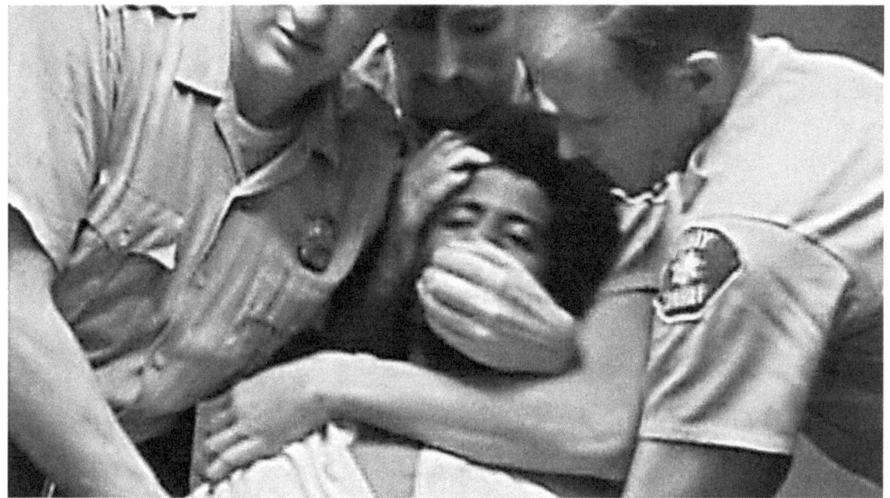

Figure 4: Punishment Park © "The first task of free men is to call things by their name."

The second focal point here is that free men call things by their name. In *The Room* Mr. Stills from the police department also refers to *'the Haagstromm incident'*[148], which is institutional denial and a *dis*placement of language. The frame from *Punishment Park* illustrates a vital point of intersection between the two works. The protagonists in both works are not free and they are 'victimized by *insane* and brutal authority.'[149]

> They were complete *equals*. He realized that they understood immediately that he was not just another crank, or simply paranoid, but a man wronged by the authorities. It was also evident that they understood that he was not only fighting for his own rights and vindication, but for that of others who *have been, are, and will be* abused by this same authority if something is not done to check its malignant growth.[150]

Ridenhour's letter is somewhat reminiscent of the protagonist's reverie and both emphasize the importance of *equality.* Two important points arise from this reverie of the protagonist and the first is that his reverie is a kind of representation

148 {see Selby, The Room, p. 171}

149 {see Selby, The Room, p. 114}

150 {see Selby, The Room, pp. 10-11. [italics mine]}

and spectacle. "In societies where modern conditions of production prevail, all of life presents itself as an immense accumulation of spectacles. Everything that was directly lived has moved away into a representation."[151] The protagonist prefers to perceive himself in a representation of himself. His reveries are some kind of spectacle and he sees himself through this *dis*tortion. One of his reveries becomes for the protagonist more than just an image or something conjured up in his mind. It becomes more real than the cell in which he was locked yet did not exist.[152] Thus the real is abolished. Barthes states the spectacle is a place where the Other threatens to appear in full view. This space becomes a mirror because the Other is a scandal, which threatens the essence of the petit-bourgeois.[153] The protagonist does not want to see his own Otherness and thus the spectacle functions as a mirror that distorts his perception of himself. The second important point is his fight is not solely for himself but also for those who *'have been, are, and will be'* wronged by authority. *The Room* is dedicated with love to the thousands who remain nameless and know. An important feature of Brecht's aesthetics is the use of a character as contradiction, "a stage on which social contradictions are played out."[154] The novel is an indictment of the social contradiction that America is a nation built on inequality but maintains the *illusion of equality*. The previous quote illustrates that the protagonist is fully aware of the *illusion of equality* as he only achieves equality in his reverie. Is he really the forgotten American male or is he rather the ignored American male? David Hess, the actor who impersonated Krug, described his childhood as one of being ignored. He was on his own volition as a child and thus developed fantasies.[155] It is concluded there is a causality between being ignored and the development of reveries. What does the *omission* of his name suggest?

In *The Room* the nameless hero stands for all that are nameless and have suffered from an abuse by authority. Pierre Bourdieu points out the social world tends to identify normality with identity and the proper name is a form of nomination that institutes a constant social identity. This institution of identity in the sense of self-identity is a requirement by the social order. The proper name can only attest to the identity of a personality, which is a socially constituted individuality and thus leads to an *enormous abstraction*. Bourdieu concludes the

151 {see Guy Debord, Society of the Spectacle (Detroit 1983), p. 1}

152 {see Selby, The Room, p. 65}

153 {see Barthes, Selected, p. 141}

154 {see Stam, Film, p. 146}

155 {see Craven, The Last House on the Left}

proper name is the support of social identity and it is the true object of these acts of attribution, which are operated under the control of the State.[156] The protagonist strives in his fantasies to be no longer an unknown, insignificant and impotent nobody who is shoved around by sadistic slobs and an impersonal law.[157] Selby portrays the character of the protagonist with a clarity that would be destroyed by the *enormous abstraction* that a proper name would entail. The omission of a name signifies the rejection of equating normality with identity and of the requirements of the social order. *Furthermore, the nameless individual is a way of evading the control of the State.*

"We all *obey* the law. The law is simply and solely made for the *exploitation* of those who do not understand it or of those who, for naked need, cannot *obey* it."[158] Brecht brings together obedience, exploitation and the law and it will be illustrated that this chain of reasoning is also found in *The Room*. There is a similarity between a quote from Michel Foucault and Selby, which is an anchorage point here. "Is it surprising that prisons resemble factories, schools, barracks, hospitals, which all resemble prisons?" Foucault argues the hospital, the school, or the workshop can become apparatuses through discipline. Any mechanism of objectification can be used in them as an *instrument of subjection.*[159] "What I mean is, there are all forms of abuses of authority – police, politicians, unions, bankers, schools, prisons – and god knows how many others." The protagonist thinks about how to expose authoritative evils in the world without people becoming immune to such a campaign.[160] Selby traces the abuse of authority in the different apparatuses and faces the predicament of exposing authoritative evils without an inoculation effect. How are the *instruments of subjection* employed and what are their effects?

Foucault outlines there are two phases of the *seizure of power*. First, over the body in an individualizing mode and second in a massifying mode that is directed at man-as-species.[161] Disciplinary tactics are situated on the axis that links the singular and the multiple and constitute the base of *'cellular power.'* The disciplinary space is always cellular and its organization is at once architectural, functional and hierarchical which makes these spaces *real and ideal* at the

---

156 {see Du Gay, Identity, pp. 301-303}

157 {see Selby, The Room, p. 62}

158 {see Bertolt Brecht, The Threepenny Opera, p. 74}

159 {see Foucault, Discipline, p. 224}

160 {see Selby, The Room, p. 30}

161 {see Gregg, The Affect, p. 222}

same time. Cellular power is a disciplinary tactic, which allows the characterization of the individual as individual as well as the ordering of a given multiplicity. *Cellular* is a characteristic of the individual created by discipline out of the control over the body.[162] With the shift of reality and fiction the cellular space has become an internal space that is *real and ideal*. Prison-existence serves here as an allegory for the subjection of the mind as well as the body. This seizure of power is projected on the *universal individual* and thus illustrates the individualizing mode as well as the massifying mode. The aim of this cellular space is to increase the obedience of the subject as well as to manipulate a given multiplicity. According to Foucault, all authorities that exercise individual control function according binary division. They decide who is mad and who is sane, who is normal and who is abnormal.[163] The protagonist refers repeatedly to a game they played when he was a child, which is cops and robbers. Selby combines the metaphor of the game with binary division and thus mirrors the mechanism of the moral superstructure. Towards the end of the novel the protagonist is beat and realizes: "Cops or robbers, robbers or cops. Its all the same. A big nothing."[164] Binary division does no longer exist for the protagonist who realizes the gap between meaning and words. He was raised with an awareness of binary division and the purpose of this awareness was exploitation. The novel reveals the gulf between word and object and thus destroys the Manichean aesthetic of the system of power.

"The whole rotten system. By the time I'm finished with them everyone will know how rotten the system is. I/ll beat them at their own game."[165] The protagonist combines the notion of a rotten system with the metaphor of the game, which was encountered in the last two chapters, and this repetition is rather peculiar. The expression 'to beat them at their own game' is read as a strategy to employ the *means of alienation* against alienation. The protagonist sees himself in a position with no option for victory but only for submission. He realizes in the end of the novel that he just cannot win.[166] As in *Punishment Park* this game is not designed to be won but to exploit. "And in the end the *game of power* becomes nothing but the critical obsession with power – obsession with its death,

162 {see Foucault, Discipline, pp. 143, 148, 149, 167}

163 {see Foucault, Discipline, p. 199}

164 {see Selby, The Room, p. 181}

165 {see Selby, The Room, p. 17}

166 {see Selby, The Room, pp. 193, 224}

obsession with its survival, which increases as it disappears."[167] The protagonist is obsessed with the *game of power* and his desire to win is self-destructive. Thoreau states that under a government that imprisons any unjustly the true place for a just man is also a prison.[168] The quote is reminiscent of the lines from *Punishment Park.* Watkins as well as Thoreau both point out that the American government imprisons unjustly and fails to imprison justly. This is only partial true for the protagonist as he may not have committed a crime but he is nevertheless guilty. Selby outlines the tragedy of this man is that he has found himself guilty.[169] This is the reason there is no escape for him. The protagonist states with the lack of consciousness come dreams of wakefulness.[170] Giles states Selby outlines the internal landscape of a single human consciousness.[171] This argument pursues the idea Selby actually outlines the consciousness of a universal individual which represents America and its *collective guilt* which is the tolerance of authoritative evils.

Hugo describes drama as a mirror that reflects nature. It is a fact that color and light are lost in a simple reflection. He concludes drama needs to be *un miroir de concentration.* This kind of mirror gathers the colored rays and *condenses* them instead of weakening them. The colored rays turn a glimmer of light into light; they turn light into a flame.[172] *The Room* also functions as *un miroir de concentration* and condenses the power of the work through its abstractedness. According to Barthes, in a strong myth the political quantum is immediate and the *de*politicization is abrupt whereas in a weak myth the political quality of the object has faded like a color. The slightest thing can bring back its strength brutally.[173] Selby creates a counter-myth with *The Room* and his politicization is made abrupt by the grotesque and the sublime. The protagonist states sometimes he feels like a motherless child.[174] But the only motherless child in the novel is Mrs. Haagstromm's daughter which raises the question what the connection is between the protagonist and Mrs. Haagstromm. This brings us back to Priest and magic as metaphor. "… I have *omitted* the significant information, and now you

167 {see Baudrillard, Simulation, p. 23}

168 {see Thoreau, Civil, p. 9}

169 {see Giles, Understanding, p. 68}

170 {see Selby, The Room, p. 195}

171 {see Giles, Understanding, p. 45}

172 {see Hugo, Cromwell, p. 90}

173 {see Barthes, Barthes, p. 133}

174 {see Selby, The Room, p. 224}

are looking in the wrong place."[175] Allegory is the *art of omission*, simplification and suggestion. It is a shape constantly re-articulating itself and is puzzling like a rebus.[176] The connection between the two is *omitted* intentionally in order to make it more abstract and *enigmatic*. So the focus is not laid on their relations to each other but to power. The actual center of the novel is the rape and destruction of Mrs. Haagstromm. The book has 225 pages and the painful elaborate description of the rape starts at page 100 and ends at page 110. Although the dog training of the two officers began before the rape 'the performance before a select audience' takes place after the rape. The protagonist describes the things they did to her are beyond human imagination and that only an evil animal could conceive of doing such things. "*What threatens the least of us threatens all of us.*" He underlines that any helpless individual may be the victim of brutal authority. He states that she is but one and he is but one. One that they know about and asks what about the thousands who remain unknown. Later in the novel he refers to his crusade with 'my – our.'[177] Both had to endure police brutality but his past is very vague and obscure whereas Mrs. Haagstromm's *plight* is immensely detailed. It is also the only section in the book in which he is absent. It is not his memory, it is not his reverie but what is it? It is more important to him to gain retribution for her than for him. The name Haagstromm can be read as an anagram for 'math' and 'orgasm.' These two words stand for the body and mind schism. It is argued that Mrs. Haagstromm represents the Cartesian split and the destruction of her body directly triggers the destruction of her mind.

Giles outlines the novel investigates the sources and origins of a truly *insane* level of misogyny. He also recommends reading the abstract violent passages of the novel in specific context of Nazi atrocities, which showed that no human atrocity is unthinkable.[178] This argument holds the position that it is more advisable to include the context of war crimes in Vietnam which also showed that no human atrocity is unthinkable. Selby chose to combine the elements crime and sex in order to illustrate a crucial transfer point of relations of power. This strategy is also read as a way to bring the war out there home. The protagonist states it might happen to your wife, your mother or your daugther.[179] That is exactly what Craven did in *The Last House* as Krug also raped and tortured the daughter

175 {see Priest, The Prestige, p. 34}

176 {see Tambling, Allegory, p. 160}

177 {see Selby, The Room, pp. 112, 114, 115, 176}

178 {see Giles, Understanding, p. 47, 51, 66}

179 {see Selby, The Room, p. 114}

of the Collingwoods. *The Room* thematizes not misogyny but *war crimes* and what happens to a society that ignores them. The novel emphasizes the *insane* level of authoritative violence and the only option to oppose this *insanity* is a *commitment to sanity.*

The crescendo of the novel is the public performance in *the abstract room* from which the title is derived. The protagonist wants to demonstrate to the families of his dogs that he is the 'worlds greatest dog trainer.' This public performance is supposed to reveal what would otherwise never be revealed: *the submission of forces and bodies /the molding of reflexively obedient killers.* The aim is to disrupt the apathy of the audience, to disrupt the big, quiet nothing in the room. Three points of views are distinguished in the room: oppressor, oppressed and silent audience (majority). The audience has to acknowledge the inhuman extent of *the molding of reflexively obedient killers.* Baudrillard outlines the mass is aware that there is no liberation and that a system is abolished only by pushing it into hyperlogic, by forcing it into an excessive practice which is equivalent to a brutal *amortization.*[180] The public performance is read as an excessive practice and what Baudrillard terms *amortization* is termed in the novel *retribution.* According to Nietzsche, every sufferer instinctively seeks a cause for his suffering, a guilty agent. He has a desire to deaden pain by *means of affect.* When a secret pain becomes unendurable he wants to drive it out of consciousness at least for the moment. This requires an affect as savage as possible.[181] Barthes states the speech of the oppressed is poor and monotonous. His language is only that of his actions and metalanguage is an inaccessible luxury. The speech of the oppressed is real and he has only one language, that of his emancipation whereas the oppressor has an exclusive right to metalanguage.[182] The protagonist becomes the oppressor in his reveries of *retribution* and thus gains access to a rich metalanguage. Selby creates an immense affect with the protagonist's *sublime joy* in terror. The joy of the protagonist is antithetical to the pain of his dogs.

> "And o god, it was good to feel their desperation and *hopelessness*. To see the pain not only in their eyes, but in the very flesh and muscle and sinew of their bodies. *And the more he felt the painful immobility of their time, the more time, for him, was non-existent and sublime.*"[183]

---

180 {see Baudrillard, In the Shadow, p. 65}

181 {see Gelder, The Horror, p. 107}

182 {see Barthes, Selected, p. 137-138}

183 {see Selby, The Room, p. 76 [italics mine]}

The terror he produces affects their inside as well as their outside, which is vital for his *sublime joy.* A court-appointed psychiatrist described that the two officers would experience *extreme emotional elation* from committing cruel acts and they would feel *justified* in committing such acts.[184] The term *justified* is reminiscent of the expression *'justified for military reasons'*, which *masked* lawlessness in the Americal Division. Selby translates the *extreme emotional elation* into the sublime and the protagonist refers on three occasions to his pleasure as sublime. "... he tingled and vibrated with the old exquisite joy and he suddenly jerked his head toward the audience and instantaneously absorbed their horrifying apprehension and this joy became sublime."[185] Sublime pleasure can only be achieved before an audience, which in this case is represented, by the families of his dogs. *His aim is to drive out consciousness but with the lack of consciousness come dreams of wakefulness.* Jean-Luc Nancy describes in *L'Offrande Sublime* the sublime as an extraordinary sentiment of the subject, which borders on the limits of experience. The sublime is not pleasurable without being painful at the same moment. According to Kant, this constitutes the *affective character of the sublime*. It is a border experience and thus signifies a *lack of emotion* (sentiment insensible). It is not determined by pleasure or pain but by pleasure and pain affecting one another. This unique ambivalence results in a moment of apatheia (syncope du sentiment).[186] But a moment of apatheia cannot render the protagonist his desired escape. Hugo outlines the modern muse feels that the grotesque exists together with the sublime. Poetry has the task to blend the grotesque and the sublime, the body and the soul. The grotesque with regard to the sublime is a *means of contrast* and the richest source offered by nature to art. The grotesque is a moment of reflection, and a point of departure from which a new perspective can be gained on the beautiful.[187] In *The Room* this position is reversed as the beautiful is used in order to gain a new perspective on the grotesque. Hugo states the sublime and the grotesque produce all kinds of effects. On the one hand they produce abstract vices, ridiculousness and on the other hand they produce abstract crimes, valor and virtues.[188] *Within the line of this argument the sublime and the grotesque produce the abstract passion terror.*

184 {see Selby, The Room, p. 173}
185 {see Selby, The Room, p. 165}
186 {see Courtine, Du Sublime, pp. 78-82}
187 {see Hugo, Cromwell, pp. 69, 72}
188 {see Hugo, Cromwell, p. 79}

A look at the film *Salò o Le 120 Giornate di Sodoma* (1975) by Pier Paolo Pasolini will illustrate the last focal points. Roberto Chiesi outlines that in *Salò* four monstrous men (a duke, a bishop, a magistrate, and a president) humiliate, torture and kill young men and women who did not manage to adapt to the new order that is imposed by the four monsters. Hell becomes a hallucinatory space of torture and loathsome acts. This vision of hell is a mere performance space in which the spectacle mirrors the reality of actions carried out in it. Chiesi points out *Salò* refers to the destruction of Italian culture by mass conformity imposed by petit-bourgeois models in the 1970s. The domination of television and consumerism reached all areas of Italian society. The films apocalyptic vision depicts a society in which there is *no hope of transformation.*[189] In *Salò*, Pasolini also refers to the sublime by quoting the German poet Gottfried Benn.[190] *The Room* is also a hallucinatory space that alludes to something else and is connected to *Salò* via the sublime.

Other points of intersection are *inhuman cruelty* and the notion of *hopelessness*. The protagonist in *The Room* describes himself as *hope for the hopeless* and Mrs. Haagstromm is *hopelessly* insane.[191] The protagonist and the Duke in *Salò* indulge in the pleasure of the sublime through terror. The Duke states he can only rejoice when he sees others are degraded. Only when others suffer humiliating disdain can he experience the exquisite pleasure of realizing how much better it is to be him instead of being part of what he regards as the human scum. "Wherever men are *equal* and such differences do not exist, true happiness can never exist."[192] Both works explore a reality that is founded on difference and where equality is only an illusion. The protagonist in *The Room* describes the performance in the *abstract room* as the beautiful terror of the game and his experience as the deep joy of controlling everything that was happening to all in the room. "Never had he experienced such infinite power and excruciating joy..."[193] The *game of power* is depicted as a means of control which produces joy on the part of the oppressor.

The protagonist adds sex (sodomy) to the public performance in the *abstract room* in order to *dis*rupt the apathy of the audience. Foucault states the master of discipline and the subject communicate via a precise system of command. The

---

189 {see Pasolini, Pasolini, pp. 102-103, 199}

190 {see Pier Paolo Pasolini, Salò o le 120 giornate di Sodoma (1975)}

191 {see Selby, The Room, pp. 67, 115}

192 {see Pasolini, Salò}

193 {see Selby, The Room, pp. 158-159}

subject perceives a signal and reacts immediately to it. The body is situated in a *world of signals,* which is a technique of training that demands prompt and blind obedience. Any appearance of indocility is regarded as a crime. Examination is highly ritualized in the mechanisms of discipline. It manifests the subjection of those who are perceived as objects and the objectification of those who are subjected.[194] The protagonist describes pain as an effective teacher in the training program of the dogs. He refers to different phases of the indoctrination. "A dog should be able to survive no matter what the circumstances." He also points out that he wants healthy dogs and so the examinations were extremely painful. He describes his dogs as different from most other dogs but as the sexual drive in all animals is strong he assumes it is proper to teach them how to screw.[195]

Figure 5: Salò © Selby and Pasolini both depict the submission of forces and bodies via the metaphor of dog training

The protagonist is the master of discipline and situates the bodies of his dogs in a *world of signals*. The examinations are supposed to manifest their subjection. Pasolini also creates a *world of signals* through the metaphor of dog training as the frame illustrates. Sex is a key element in *Salò* and in a discussion between the Duke and the Bishop they argue about sodomy versus execution. The Duke emphasizes that *sodomy signifies death* and transgresses social standards.

194 {see Foucault, Discipline, pp. 166, 184-185}

195 {see Selby, The Room, pp. 72-73, 79, 81-82}

He prefers sodomy to execution as it has the advantage of *repetition.*[196] Giles points out that sex for male characters in Selby's work is linked with death rather than with life.[197] Two important points arise with regard to sodomy.

First, in *The Room* a graphic depiction of sodomy is used to illustrate the utmost level of exploitation as well as subjection. Jacques Lacan outlines the anal level is a *space of metaphor* where one object (phallus) is substituted for another (excrement). The anal drive is the realm of sacrifice, offering, present. Where due to lack one cannot give one always has the possibility to give something else. This is the reason why man as a moral being belongs to the realm of the anal, which is most true for the materialist.[198] The representation of the dogs' animalistic desire is supposed to show the audience (their families) the extent of their subjection and the ensuing inhumanity that is generated by blind obedience. The previous frame from *Salò* also underlines the effect of subjection. Ballard states pornography is in a sense the most political form of fiction. It deals with how people exploit each other in the most ruthless way.[199] Pornography in *The Room* is read as a political form of fiction. Sexuality as a transfer point of relations is a means for control. The novel illustrates *the submission of forces and bodies /the molding of reflexively obedient killers,* which the following quote exemplifies: “Nose and tongue sought out and thoroughly investigated asshole with complete acceptance. There was nothing to fight. There was no desire to fight. Through *submission to pain and exhaustion* they simply, automatically, did what they were trained to do.”[200]

Second, the repetitive character of sodomy is important. According to Foucault, the ideal point of penalty today would be an *indefinite discipline.* Disciplinary punishment favors punishments that are exercise and thus *repetitive*. Punishment and gratification constitute a double system in discipline. Behavior and performance are measured with regard to the opposed values of good and evil.[201] In the abstract reality of *The Room* there are no opposed values of good and evil. The protagonist punishes *dis*obedience and gratification is non-existent. He outlines during the dog training there was nothing as reward but only death or survival.[202] The Bishop instructs a subject that death won't be as easy as being

196 {see Pasolini, Salò}

197 {see Giles, Understanding, p. 56}

198 {see Jacques Lacan, Die Vier Grundbegriffe der Psyoanalyse (Weinheim 1987), p. 110}

199 {see Ballard, Crash, Introduction}

200 {see Selby, The Room, p. 167}

201 {see Foucault, Discipline, pp. 227, 179- 180}

202 {see Selby, The Room, p. 161}

killed. His intention is to kill the subject a thousand times over and over again until the end of eternity.[203] The Bishop and the protagonist punish over and over again in an endless procedure. Their behavior is completely inhuman and the repetitiveness of the punishment renders any hope for change utterly futile. The means of alienation in *The Room* and *Salò* are inhuman and those who employ them become inhuman, too.

> Action from principle, - the perception and the performance of right,- *changes* things and relations; it is essentially revolutionary, and does not consist wholly with any thing which was. It not only divides states and churches, it divides families; aye, it *divides the individual*, separating the diabolical in him from the divine. Unjust laws exist: shall we be content to obey them, or shall we endeavor to amend them, and obey them until we have succeeded, or shall we transgress them at once?[204]

For Henry Miller, a marriage between ideas and actions exists. Ideas are not restricted to the *vacuum of the mind*; they need to be translated into living.[205] The protagonist of *The Room* can perceive right but cannot perform right. His reveries about retribution only exist in the *vacuum of his mind* and thus the connection between ideas and actions is broken. "The more he struggled against the pressures the more *imprisoned* he became. The more enmeshed he became in their conflicting directions. The further he was tugged in opposite directions that kept him *immobile*. And the harder he fought for movement, any movement, the more stationary became his position, the more painful his existence." On the last pages of the novel the protagonist describes the sickness he feels as his friend. He describes the feeling of something rotting inside of him and that he cannot get rid of the foul taste in the back of his throat. *He states the way he feels now is the way he always felt and will always feel.*[206] The conflicting directions of American society result in the *imprisonment of the mind*. Prison-existence is here allegorical for an *immobile state of mind* and represents the narrow limits within which the protagonist is allowed to suffer. The inherent irreconcilability of values within American society makes the protagonist sick in a literal sense.

> For the very end of myths is to *immobilize* the world: they must suggest and mimic a universal order which has fixated once and for all the hierarchy of possessions. Thus, every day and everywhere, man is *stopped by myths*, referred by them to this *motionless prototype* which lives in his place, stifles him in the manner of a *huge in-*

203 {see Pasolini, Salò}

204 {see Thoreau, Civil, p. 7}

205 {see Miller, The Obelisk, p. 117}

206 {see Selby, The Room, pp. 194, 211-212, 219-221}

> *ternal parasite* and assigns to his activity the narrow limits within which he is allowed to suffer without upsetting the world: bourgeois pseudo-physis is in the fullest sense a prohibition for man against inventing himself.[207]

The protagonist has internalized the *eternalizing mode of oppression* and he has succumbed to it. He embodies the *motionless prototype* that is *immobilized* by a universal order. But as he cannot escape unconscious wakefulness he is aware of the *huge internal parasite* and it is this awareness that tortures him over and over again.

According to de Man, allegory recognizes the impossibility of saying what is intended and thus its *clarity of representation* is not linked with something that can be represented.[208] Giles points out *The Room* foregrounds the legacy of American optimism and idealism only to deny it at the end.[209] Optimism and idealism are principles as well as American myths, which differ greatly from reality with regard to war crimes during the Vietnam war. They were replaced by guilt and terror. The *clarity of representation* in the novel translates the realization of this replacement.

---

207 {see Barthes, Selected, p. 145}

208 {see Tambling, Allegory, p. 129}

209 {see Giles,Understanding, p. 50}

A Body Confused with Technology in its Violating and Violent Dimension

An Analysis of Commodified Relationships

> The soft machine is the human body under constant *siege* from a *vast and hungry host of parasites* with many names but one nature being hungry and one intention to eat. [...] You see junk *is* death the oldest 'visitor' in the industry.[210]

Henry Miller states the body follows after the mind. It gets particularly difficult when the two start going in opposite directions.[211] The perception of the right is tied to the mind and the performance of the right is tied to the body. The performance can bring about change and is threatening any existing order so the body is the first target of a siege as without the body no change can be brought about. Reynold Humphries outlines the interaction and interdependence of body (human) and technology (economic relations) are inextricably tied up with the representation and function of these twin themes.[212] The second part of this argument traces a shift towards the representation and function of these twin themes in American literature and film during the late seventies. The basic assumption is that the aim of this interaction and interdependence is *identity theft*. The *dis*tortion of the perception of the right is the second target of the siege. "I realized that the human inhabitants of this technological landscape no longer provided its sharpest pointers, its keys to the borderzones of identity."[213] The inhabitants of the works under discussion are part of a technological landscape and the task is to find out how the borderzones of identity are obliterated?

Benjamin describes melancholy as the medium through which allegory is discovered. He connects melancholy to an alienated state. Allegory does not work with *natural relationships* between things and furthermore questions such a possibility.[214] Identity theft is an alienated state and thus connected to melancholy. Allegory is a suitable device to explore human and economic relations as it depicts non-natural relations. According to Barthes, myth abolishes the complexity of human acts and it gives them the simplicity of essences, it does away

210 {see William S. Burroughs, The Soft Machine (London 1970), p. 172. [italics mine]}

211 {see Miller, The Obelisk, p. 248}

212 {see Reynold Humphries, American Horror Film: An Introduction (Edinburgh 2005), p. 185}

213 {see Ballard, Crash, p. 36}

214 {see Tambling, Allegory, pp. 110, 114}

with all dialectics. The world enters language as a dialectical relationship between human actions and it comes out of myth as a harmonious display of essences. He states a *conjuring trick* has taken place as myth turns reality inside out. Myth empties reality of history (world) and fills it with Nature (image of the world). Myth removes from things their human meaning so as to make them signify a human insignificance.[215] This *conjuring trick* with regard to Vonnegut's quote that we 'are healthy only to the extent that our ideas are humane'[216] renders an emerging image visible: Myth undoes the humanity of ideas and consequently makes people sick. One defendant from *Punishment Park* states the truth in America is that America is a sick society.[217] Selby's intent is to examine the disease of a lack of love in America. He states a spiritual emptiness permeates every economic level of American society.[218] Sickness as metaphor was already present in the first part of this argument but it is the center of attention in the second part. The metaphor of the disease reflects the spiritual emptiness and is interwoven with economy in American society during the late seventies.

"The opportunities of living are diminished in proportion as what are called the 'means' are increased."[219] Thoreau describes that the *means of living* and the *opportunities of living* are essentially opposed to each other. Capitalism employs myth as a type of speech in order to veil this antithetical relation. Tania Modleski outlines that instead of liberating humanity by freeing it from burdensome toil the proliferation of dead labor (technology) has resulted in the *invasion* of the people's mental, moral, and emotional lives. It has rendered people incapable of desiring social change.[220] As allegory is the art of rendering abstract ideas visible via substitution this invasion of people's minds is expressed via the metaphor of sickness. Brecht's *Mahagonny* engages with key aspects of contemporary capitalism and focuses on the ubiquity and omnipotence of money. It is furthermore an indictment of commodified relationships and a critique of consumer capitalism.[221] Stam states the polysemic term postmodernism implies the global ubiquity of market culture, a new stage of capitalism in which culture and information become key terrains for struggle.[222] This section of the argument

215 {see Barthes, Selected, p. 128-132}
216 {see Vonnegut, Breakfast, p. 16}
217 {see Watkins, Punishment Park}
218 {see Giles, Understanding, p. 5-6}
219 {see Thoreau, Civil, p. 10}
220 {see Gelder, The Horror, p. 282}
221 {see Brecht, Magahonny, p. vii, xxx}
222 {see Stam, Film, p. 299}

focuses on capitalism in the late seventies, explores the new key terrains for struggle and analyzes specific modalities of disciplinary power. Barthes outlines that everything in everyday life is steeped in an *anonymous ideology* that stems from the press, films, theater, rituals, justice and so on. Everything is dependent on the representation which the bourgeoisie has as well as makes people have of the relations between them and the world. Barthes emphasizes the basic idea of a perfectible mobile world produces the *inverted image* of an unchanging humanity which is characterized by an *indefinite repetition of its identity.*[223] Allegory as a *mirror de concentration* renders the *dis*tortion of an inverted image visible and renders the whole spectrum of the ideological tangible.

What happens to "a body confused with technology in its violating and violent dimension?"[224] According to Marx, colonialism can be compared to capitalism and he describes capitalism as being stripped of the decorous clothing of European society. Sartre explains colonialism consists of a process in which uncontrolled violence is transformed into controlled violence. The Manichean system of colonization only appears to divide colonizer and colonized. But actually this system creates 'dynamic mutual mental relations' between colonizer and colonized.[225] The 'dynamic mutual mental relations' become visible in a body confused with technology, which signifies the breakdown of Manichean aesthetics. According to Baudrillard, technology is never grasped except in the violence done to the body.[226] It is concluded *controlled violence* is an essential part of the *relations of power* under capitalism. Foucault outlines that the growth of a capitalist economy gave rise to the specific modality of disciplinary power whose techniques of *submitting forces and bodies* could be operated in the most diverse political régimes, apparatuses or institutions.[227] How are specific modalities of disciplinary power and the rise of capitalism interconnected?

Lukács points out that any accurate account of reality is a contribution to the Marxist critique of capitalism.[228] He states the fictional world produced by authors corresponds to the Marxist conception of the real world that consists of class conflicts, economic as well as social contradictions, and ultimately the al-

223 {see Barthes, Barthes, pp. 128-130}

224 {see Baudrillard, Simulacra, p. 111}

225 {see Jean-Paul Sartre, Colonialism and Neocolonialism (London 2006), pp. xiv, xvi, xvii}

226 {see Baudrillard, Simulacra, p. 112}

227 {see Foucault, Discipline, p.221}

228 {see Newton, Twentieth-Century, p. 90}

ienation of the individual under capitalism.[229] The works of the late seventies focus on the inhabitants of technological landscapes, i.e. the alienated individual under capitalism. The artists create allegorical works that mirror the substitution of the real with signs of the real. Their account of the signs of the real is a Marxist critique of capitalism.

> Capital, in fact, was never linked by a contract to the society that it dominates. It is a *sorcery of social relations*, it is a challenge to society, and it must be responded as such. It is not a scandal to be denounced according to moral or economic rationality, but a challenge to take up according to symbolic law.[230]

Selby dedicates his novel *Requiem for a Dream* to four individuals who did not knew '*the difference between the Vision in their hearts and the illusion of the American Dream.*' He describes the illusion as a lie, which makes the truth of their vision inaccessible and ultimately culminates in the loss of all values. Selby believes that to pursue the American Dream is not only futile but also *self-destructive*. This pursuit destroys everything and everyone involved with it and by definition it must. It nurtures everything except those things that are important like integrity, truth, our very heart and soul.[231] What Selby terms the *illusion of the American Dream* is what Baudrillard terms the imaginary concealing that no reality exists outside than inside the limits of the artificial perimeter. According to Baudrillard, capital functions behind a moral superstructure and in reviving public morality the order of capital is strengthened.[232] The works under discussion realize that capital is a *sorcery of social relations* and take up the challenge according to symbolic law. They understand that *self-destruction* is a vital element in a discussion about American society in the late seventies. “Our awareness is all that is alive and maybe sacred in any of us. Everything else about us is dead machinery.”[233] This is the very reason they appeal to the awareness of people with enigmatic images as even *with the lack of consciousness come dreams of wakefulness.*

229 {see Abrams, A Glossary, p. 243}

230 {see Baudrillard, Simulacra, p. 15}

231 {see Hubert Selby, Jr., Requiem for a Dream (New York 2000), p. v-vi}

232 {see Baudrillard, Simulacra, p. 14}

233 {see Kurt Vonnegut, Breakfast of Champions or Goodbye Blue Monday! (New York 1999), 226}

A Scanner Darkly (1977)

> The music from the clock radio is to wake you up; the music from the junkie is to get you to become a means for him to obtain more junk, in whatever way you can serve. He, a machine, will turn you into *his* machine. Every junkie, he thought, is a recording. [234]

The quote from *A Scanner Darkly* (1977) by Philip K. Dick introduces the focal points of this section. The quote illustrates that relations of power function through objectification and commodified relationships. David Cronenberg points out that in North America as a Science Fiction writer you are regarded as a second or third-class writer. It is not a matter of how extraordinary your ideas or your literary style are. For him Philip K. Dick's work is *de*valued because the Science Fiction genre is *de*valued in the West in general.[235] Fredric Jameson outlines in *Philip K. Dick, In Memoriam* that a mass-cultural sub-genre like Science Fiction can sometimes express realities and dimensions that escape high literature.[236] The first section of this argument illustrated how powerful a combination between genre and allegory works with regard to abstract ideas. In *A Scanner Darkly* we encounter the use of the Science Fiction genre and the allegory of addiction. Addiction is substituted in order to illustrate hidden power relations in American society during the late seventies. For Burroughs, *money is like junk.* The concept of money is that it always takes more and more to buy less and less. It is the same with junk as a dose that fixes on Monday won't fix on Friday.[237] Junk incorporates many connotations and one is the comparison to money.

Dick states in the author's note that the novel is about some people who were punished because they continued *to play* and compares them to children who played in the street. Drug misuse is a decision of a set of people and thus becomes a social error (a life-style). He points out the novel is not bourgeois and has no moral, it just narrates the consequences. "I myself, I am not a character in this novel; I am the novel. So, though, was our entire nation at this time."[238] Two vital points emerge here. First, the reference to 'our entire nation at this time' situates the novel in a historical and social context. Jameson outlines that Science

234 {see Philip K. Dick, A Scanner Darkly (New York 2006), p. 159}

235 {see Cronenberg, Interviews, p. 40}

236 {see Fredric Jameson, Archaeologies of the Future: The Desire called Utopia and other Science Fictions (New York 2007), p. 345}

237 {see William S. Burroughs, Exterminator (New York 1979), 101}

238 {see Dick, A Scanner, pp. 276-278}

Fiction is widely understood as an attempt to imagine unimaginable futures but at its core may actually be the historical present.[239] Second, Dick distinguishes his work from bourgeois concepts of morality and thus from bourgeois value systems, from the morality of behaviors. Lejla Kucukalic states in *Philip K. Dick: Canonical Writer of the Digital Age* that two questions are central to Dick's work: what is human and what is real.[240] The questions of humanity and reality also have been part of this argument so far. According to Baudrillard, there are three orders of simulacra and the second order corresponds to Science Fiction. He admits the three orders may interfere with each other at the level of Science Fiction but emphasizes only the third order is of interest for him. The third order is founded on information, the model, the cybernetic *game*, total operationality and hyperreality. This order directly aims at total control.[241] Addiction is a strong metaphor to exemplify the aim of total control. First, control is exerted over the body and then over the mind. It is argued that *A Scanner Darkly* functions via the third order because it is a world of signs.

The protagonist Robert Arctor is an undercover narcotics agent in California. Arctor describes life in Anaheim as a commercial for itself, which is replayed endlessly as nothing ever changed. Once he had a wife, two daughters and a house but he hated his life as it was too safe. “It was like, he had once thought, a little plastic boat that would sail on forever, without incident, until it finally sank, which would be a secret relief to all.” He left his life behind and entered this dark world in which he could count on nothing.[242] The term 'sail on forever, without incident,' indicates monotony and an unchanging humanity Arctor had to escape. The term 'little plastic boat' signifies an artificial and confined space. The combination between monotony and artificiality incited him to seek a life full of darkness. As an undercover agent he has to conceal his identity and thus has to wear a scramble suit while talking to other agents. The wearer of a scramble suit is Everyman and looks like a vague blur. He cannot be identified by voice or appearance. Robert Arctor's code name as an agent is Fred and his name as an addict is Bob. His new assignment is to primarily observe Bob Arctor, i. e. himself. “What is identity? he asked himself. Where does the act

239 {see Jameson, Archaeologies of the Future, p. 345}

240 {see Lejla Kucukalic, Philip K. Dick: Canonical Writer of the Digital Age (New York 2009), p. 2}

241 {see Baudrillard, Simulacra, pp. 121, 126, 127}

242 {see Dick, A Scanner, p. 31, 64}

end? Nobody knows."[243] Thomas Hobbes states the Latin word Persona signifies disguise or outward appearance of a man counterfeited on the Stage. A Person is the same as an Actor and to Personate is to Act, to Represent himself or an other. He defines the word prosopopoeia as the mask (disguise) the actor puts on. The conclusion is that *to act is allegorical* and speaking the words of another on stage or in any social interaction is acting. The *mask* covers the face and thus allegory is inseparable form questions of disguise, false seeming and hypocrisy.[244] Arctor himself makes the connection between Actor and his name Arctor.[245] Kucukalic argues that the scramble suit is a metaphor for Arctor's loss of identity that begins physical and later becomes spiritual.[246] This argument pursues the idea that the scramble suit is a metaphor for the act to 'nullify yourself.' Arctor's loss of identity stems from his two contradicting life styles and the massive drug abuse. De Man argues prosopopoeia originates in mourning which includes melancholy. It creates something, which is only a mask, a *state of loss* that produces the *illusion of a real other person through the power of allegory.*[247] *"How many Bob Arctors are there?"* Arctor counts two that he can think of and asks himself if Fred actually is the same as Bob? He is the only person who actually knows that Fred is Bob Arctor. "*But*, he thought, *who am I? Which of them is me?"*[248] The *illusion of a real other person* originates in Arctor's lost sense of identity. Which of both is his real identity and which is the artificial identity? Which of these two personae has substituted the other? Bertolt Brecht describes the character Brown, the Chief of Police in *The Threepenny Opera,* as a very modern phenomenon. His character is essentially split, as the private being is different from the official being. "And this is not a dichotomy *in spite of* which he lives, but one *because of* which he lives. And beside him, the whole society lives through this dichotomy of his." The private being is opposed to the official being as both act against the conviction of the other. Brecht's conclusion is that Life soils everything.[249] Arctor and Brown share this dichotomy and represent a collective state of mind. Arctor's split between Bob and Fred illustrates two opposed modes of living. One is shaped by bourgeois myths and the other has the capacity to perceive things as they really are. But exactly this capacity is

243 {see Dick, A Scanner, pp. 22-23, 29}

244 {see Tambling, Allegory, pp. 139, 140, 143}

245 {see Dick, A Scanner, p. 134}

246 {see Kucukalic, Philip K. Dick, p. 122}

247 {see Tambling, Allegory, p. 144}

248 {see Dick, A Scanner, p. 96}

249 {see Bertolt Brecht, The Threepenny Opera (New York 1964), pp. 102-103}

diminished with his increased drug abuse. *A Scanner Darkly* functions through allegory in order to illustrate the loss of identity.

> I hope it does, he thought, see clearly. I see only murk. Murk outside; murk inside; I hope, for everyone's sake, the scanners do better. Because, he thought, if the scanner sees only darkly, the way I myself do, then we are cursed, cursed again like we have been continually, and we'll wind up dead this way, knowing very little and getting that little fragment wrong, too.[250]

The quote illustrates Arctor's vision, which is only darkly. 'Murk outside' describes the world and 'murk inside' describes his inner condition. His darkly vision is a metaphor for the loss of Manichean aesthetics. Arctor meditates on the obliteration of differences between undercover narks and addicts. Agents get deeper and deeper into using their own stuff. They become rich dealer addicts as well as narks and some phase out their law-enforcement activities in favor of full-time dealing. On the other hand some dealers wind up as sort of unofficial undercover narks. "It all got murky. The drug world was *a murky world* for everyone anyhow."[251] Selby mourns the loss of binary opposites with the metaphor of cops and robbers. Dick uses the metaphor of cops and addicts with the same aim. Kucukalic states the drug world and the straight world are not a duality but two separate entities that operate under the same rules.[252]

This argument pursues the idea the drug world (murky world) is an allegory of the straight world and its mechanisms. The drug world is *substituted* for a straight world that has lost referentiality and thus everything is murk. Arctor's friend Donna meditates on the Golden Age when wisdom and justice were the same. "Before it all shattered into cutting fragments. Into broken bits that don't fit, that can't be put back together, hard as we try."[253] Dick explores the fragmented state of the American mind during the late seventies. Although he expresses a longing for the Golden Age it cannot be retrieved. The distinction itself between drug world and straight world is an illusion created by those in power to create antagonism. "People who would burglarize your house and take your color TV are the same kind of criminals who slaughter animals or vandalize priceless work of art." This is a statement of an upper-class well-off straight couple whose furniture had been ripped off and reflects bourgeois prejudices. Arctor thinks about this statement but his own experience is the opposite. He has

250 {see Dick, A Scanner, p. 185}

251 {see Dick, A Scanner, p. 87}

252 {see Kucukalic, Philip K. Dick, p. 120}

253 {see Dick, A Scanner, p. 236}

experienced that addicts rarely hurt animals. He does not understand what the expression 'priceless work of art' is supposed to mean. "At My Lai during the Viet Nam War, four hundred and fifty priceless works of art had been vandalized to death at the orders of the CIA."[254] The repercussions of the Vietnam War and war crimes committed by the American military are present in the novel. Two different definitions of crime are encountered and confronted with each other. The straight definition of crime is to destroy material objects whereas Arctor's definition of crime is ruthless murder of civilians. The two opposing value systems are essentially antithetical. The term 'priceless work of art' is a *dis*placement of language and a *de*referentialization of the real that is absent. Mike Westway describes Arctor's feelings for Donna as being in love with a *phantom of authority.* He states God's modus operandi is to transmute evil into good in a process that lies hidden beneath the surface of reality. Donna outlines she is warm on the outside but cold on the inside. She is not what she seems to be.[255] Donna as the *phantom of authority* exemplifies that the double mode of binary dibion has broken down. The *magic trick* of authority is to create the *illusion* of this double mode, which does not exist anymore. And the Golden Age is long gone.

What does Arctor's work as a law enforcement officer signify? Foucault outlines the police apparatus is an infinitely small of political power and uses the instrument of permanent and omnipresent surveillance. This power must be capable of making all visible and remain invisible. It is a faceless gaze that transforms the whole social body into a field of perception. "The practice of placing individuals under 'observation' is a natural extension of a justice imbued with disciplinary methods and examination procedures." Bentham's principle of the Panopticon is that power should be visible and unverifiable. The Panoptic machine *dis*sociates the see/being seen dyad.[256] The 'law-enforcement apparatus' puts the house of Arctor under surveillance with complicated holo-scanners, which should never be visible. Arctor is worried about what will be on the scanners. He is convinced that whatever it is that's watching is not human. Due to the brain damage caused by Substance D he perceives the world as reflected in a darkened mirror.[257] Bob's assumption that whatever is watching is not human reveals that he is not aware that he himself is watching. Fred does not realize

254 {see Dick, A Scanner, p. 95}

255 {see Dick, A Scanner, p. 257-259}

256 {see Foucault, Discipline, pp. 213-214, 227, 201-202}

257 {see Dick, A Scanner, pp. 58, 73, 133, 185, 212}

when he sees himself on the scanner that he sees himself reversed and ultimately does not recognize himself at all. The darkened mirror makes power unverifiable. Arctor's friends do not know the scanners are there and thus power is invisible. Arctor knows the scanners are there and thus power is visible. The scanner is the instrument of power and it is visible / invisible at the same time. It is argued the scanners are an abstract embodiment of the Panoptic machine. Arctor is only an infinitely small aspect of the *game of power* whose rules elude him. Foucault further states the fact of being constantly seen maintains the disciplined individual in his subjection. Examination is a technique of power that holds the subjects in a mechanism of objectification and is consequently the ceremony of objectification.[258] The act of examination is for Arctor a task that cannot be executed by a something human. It is argued that the scanner turns *living labor* into *dead labor* through the passive act of watching. The scanner as an instrument of power transforms the examined subject as well as the examiner. Foucault outlines a real subjection is born mechanically from a *fictitious relationship*. He who is subjected to a field of visibility inscribes in himself the power relation in which he simultaneously plays both roles and thus he becomes the principle of his own subjection.[259] Arctor virtually plays both roles and becomes the principle of his own subjection. This *fictitious relationship* becomes visible in Arctor's split identity between Fred and Bob. Arctor describes the *invisibility of power* as the most effective form of industrial or military sabotage. An *invisible political movement*, which perhaps isn't there at all, makes a person assume he is paranoid and doubts himself. This wipes him out more thoroughly than anything that can be traced.[260] The nature of an *invisible political movement* is a means to achieve total control over the subject.

What does junk as a metaphor signify? Deleuze argues in the societies of control one is never finished with anything. The acquittal of the disciplinary societies and the limitless postponements of the societies of control are two different modes of juridical life.[261] The idea that one is never finished with anything corresponds to 'an indefinite discipline' as an ideal point of penalty. Arctor states an undercover narcotics agent fears most that he will roll an endless horror feature film in his head for the remainder of his life. This is the risk of a junky and

258 {see Foucault, Discipline, p.187}

259 {see Foucault, Discipline, pp. 202-203}

260 {see Dick, A Scanner, p. 91}

261 {see Gilles Deleuze, Postscript on the Societies of Control (The MIT Press Winter 1992), p. 5}

what happens to Charles Freck as he tries to commit suicide. The capsules he bought do not contain barbiturates but some kind of kinky psychedelics. He sees a creature that tells him he has been elevated to the transcendent realm where his sins will be read ceaselessly, in shifts, through eternity.[262] Mike Westaway observes that a bug sprayed with toxin dies whereas man sprayed with toxin becomes a reflex machine. For him Arctor is the saddest of all, as he has to live on past death. And what future might there be for someone who is dead? Mike states the dead who can still see are our camera.[263] Freck and Arctor both have to face a punishment that is 'beyond belief' as Dick put it in the author's note. The description of Arctor as a camera is an objectification of him and illustrates how 'dead labor' replaces 'living labor.' "Seems like the only kind of job an American can get these days is committing suicide in some way."[264] The statement 'junk is death' gains a new dimension in this context and thus Arctor's job is committing suicide in some way. But the punishment is ceaseless and transforms him into a *living dead.*

The society described in *A Scanner* is a society of control that employs disciplinary methods. Discipline is also a machinery, which adds up and capitalizes time. The 'seriation' of activities enables a detailed control and articulates power directly onto time. This seriation of time is a technique of subjection and opens up multiple dimensions of the *exercise of control* and the *practice of domination*. This procedure is called 'exercise' and it imposes on the body tasks that are repetitive and different. *Exercise connects the body with duration and tends towards a subjection that never reaches a limit.* Genetic is another characteristic of an individuality that discipline creates out of the bodies it controls. It designates the accumulation of time.[265] This seriation of time is illustrated in the theme of addiction. The nature of junk is repetitive as well as different and thus junk is a perfect tool for the exercise of power. In *A Scanner* junk is virtually a subjection that never reaches a limit as subjection goes on even beyond death. This exercise of power produces the *living dead.*

> But there was also a *political dream of the plague*, which was exactly its reverse: not the collective festival, but strict divisions; not laws transgressed, but the penetration of regulation into even the smallest details of everyday life through the mediation of the complete hierarchy that assured the capillary *functioning of power*; not masks

262 {see Dick, A Scanner, p. 188}

263 {see Dick, A Scanner, pp. 259, 265-266}

264 {see Vonnegut, Breakfast, p. 88}

265 {see Foucault, Discipline, pp. 157-158, 160-162, 167}

> that were put on and taken off, but the assignment to each individual of his 'true' name, his 'true' place, his 'true' body, his 'true' disease. The plague as a form, at once real and imaginary, of disorder had as its medical and political correlative discipline.[266]

Selby states *Requiem for a Dream* is devoted to the destructive nature of addiction and an even more widespread and more respectable kind of dependency in American life. One of the novels central characters is literally driven to insanity by her immersion in American consumerism.[267] Selby's employs addiction as an allegory for consumerism in American life and thus emphasizes the dangerous dimension of consumerism. Dick also employs addiction as an allegory for consumerism with regard to American historical and social reality. Jameson outlines Dick's novels are about business and focus on the sector of image and illusion production. His protagonists are caught in the convulsive struggles of monopoly corporations and multinationals. Dick envisions the disturbing reappearance of the collective and the so-called 'death of the subject.' For Jameson, Dick is the epic poet of drugs and pictures the absolute end to individualism.[268] It is argued that Dick is not the 'poet of drugs' but the *poet of identity theft*. According to Foucault, the aim of the Panopticon is to strengthen the social forces, to increase production, to develop the economy, and ultimately to make an apparatus of power more intense. The plague gives rise to an organization in depth of surveillance and control. It is an intensification and a ramification of power. The plague defines ideally the exercise of disciplinary power.[269] The scanners are an abstract depiction of the principle of the Panopticon and addiction is some kind of plague. Dick makes clear drug misuse is not a disease but a decision.[270] The important point is that it is *self-induced,* as the addict becomes *the principle of his own subjection*.

Patricia Clough refers to the biomediated body and states this has nothing to do with *dis*embodiment but is defined as a 'complexification in bodily matter at the molecular level as its informational capacity is made more apparent and more productive.' Biology is the process of production and replaces machines. Hence *biology is technology*.[271] Arctor states the D in Substance D stands for Dumbness, Despair, and Desertion. The "desertion of your friends from you,

266 {see Foucault, Discipline, pp. 197-198}
267 {see Giles, Understanding, p. 5}
268 {see Jameson, Archaeologies, p. 347}
269 {see Foucault, Discipline, pp. 206, 208, 198, 199}
270 {see Dick, A Scanner, p. 276}
271 {see Gregg, The Affect Theory Reader, p. 214}

you from them, everyone from everyone, isolation and loneliness and hating and suspecting each other." He concludes D stands finally for slow Death.[272] It is of utmost importance that Substance D is organic and not the product of a lab. In the end of the novel on the farm Arctor sees Substance D growing. "I saw death rising from the earth."[273] The frame from the film *A Scanner Darkly* (2006) by Richard Linklater illustrates the transcendent moment for Arctor. In *A Scanner* biology is a process of production and thus is technology.

Figure 6: A Scanner Darkly © Arctor's transcendent vision of death rising from the earth

Eugene Thacker outlines the development of genetic-specific drugs has two important points. First, to circulate the drug is necessary in order to connect information to the body and to achieve the economic gain. Second, the booming industry of diagnostic tests and the production of databases are more economic than the mere sale of drugs. *The circuit of product and effect is essential.*[274] Two points discussed with regard to *A Scanner* are how the product is put into circuit and what the effects are.

First, the product itself is of importance here. The product in *A Scanner* is Substance D and it is argued the drug can be substituted for money or death but

272 {see Dick, A Scanner, pp.26-27}

273 {see Dick, A Scanner, pp. 266, 275}

274 {see Gregg, The Affect, p. 215}

also for consumer goods. Freck describes a giant shopping mall as a fun park for grown-up kids. In the author's note Dick refers to his friends also as children playing in the street.[275] The term children entails a certain innocence on the part of the consumer / addicted but also a tendency to fall prey to temptation.

> In his *fantasy number* he was driving past the Thrifty Drugstore and they had a huge window display; bottles of slow death, cans of slow death, jars and bathtubs and vats and bowls of slow death, millions of caps and tabs and hits of slow death, slow death mixed with speed and junk and barbiturates and psychedelics, everything – and a giant sign: YOUR CREDIT IS GOOD HERE. Not to mention: LOW LOW PRICES, LOWEST IN TOWN.[276]

This quote illustrates very early in the novel the analogy between drugs and consumer goods. The fantasy number by Freck is reminiscent of the reveries of the protagonist from *The Room* but this fantasy number is dedicated to a material dream world where happiness is equated with the knowledge to have enough pills in store.[277] This kind of happiness must lead to isolation as it does not include other persons but things like drugs / consumer goods. Towards the end of the novel Substance D is termed Mors ontologica, which means death of the spirit, identity, and the essential nature.[278] Burroughs equated junk with death and Dick also takes this route but for him it means not the death of the body but the death of the mind, of the essential nature. Kucukalic states Dick feared the governmental and economic mechanism that supported a lifestyle characterized by endless production and sameness. Dick's aim is to warn against the automatic ways of living that he saw prevalent in contemporary American culture.[279] According to Deleuze, in a society of control man is no longer man enclosed but man in debt.[280] It is argued that Bruce, Arctor's new name at New-Path, embodies the man in debt who 'had too much of a good thing already.'[281] *The circulation of drugs illustrates the commodification of relationships*. Arctor explains to Donna that he gives her money and she hands him the bunch of dope. "What I mean by buy is an extension into the greater world of human business transactions of what we have present now, with us, as dope deals." He describes this transaction as a substitution for sexual relations and an even exchange until the

275 {see Dick, A Scanner, p. 11, 276 }
276 {see Dick, A Scanner, pp. 7-8 [italics mine]}
277 {see Dick, A Scanner, p. 16}
278 {see Dick, A Scanner, p. 254}
279 {see Kucukalic, Philip K. Dick, p. 131}
280 {see Deleuze, Postscript, p. 6}
281 {see Dick, A Scanner, p. 274}

hash ran out. For him that is intimacy.[282] Economic relations have substituted human relations and the absence of sexuality indicates a focus on the cerebral. Arctor has lost the capacity to recognize *the difference between the Vision in his heart and the illusion of the American Dream.*

Second, the *effect* is explored and analyzed. In *A Scanner* addiction is compared to a game board and the one goal of the addicts is the federal clinic.[283] It is interesting that in the three works discussed in the first part of this argument the notion of the game is prevalent and now it is encountered again in *A Scanner* as well as in the author's note. New-Path is a drug-rehabilitation place where everything that identifies a person is stripped away in preparation for building up a new, not drug-oriented personality. Once you go into one of these places you are dead to the world. Slogans like THE ONLY REAL FAILURE IS TO FAIL OTHERS are used by New-Path.[284] The slogan is identified as a statement of fact, one of the principal figures of Bourgeois Myths. The slogan is no longer directed toward a world to be made but overlays one which is already made. It buries the traces of this production under a self-evident appearance of eternity.[285] One concept discussed during Concept Time at New-Path is 'Motion that is circular is the deadest form of the universe.' Dick describes the circulation of the drug and the treatment of the addicts who also manufacture the drug. He creates a *dark circuit of product and effect* and illustrates the economic aspirations of New-Path. Mike knows there is a lot of money in manufacturing, distributing, and finally selling Substance D. He wonders whether New-Path sends a substance out that turns Arctor into a reflex machine so they would receive him back.[286] What Mike describes is a *dark circuit of product and effect.* The reason a circular motion is the deadest form of the universe is that it is eternal. Ideology is eternal and thus any movement, which is eternal, is part of ideology. It is important to outline that Arctor is equally and ruthlessly exploited from New-Path as well as the *phantom of authority* that is another indicator for the loss of binary distinctions in this *game of power*. The following quote from a defendant at *Punishment Park* illustrates the close connection of both works with regard to money and exploitation.

282 {see Dick, A Scanner, pp. 147, 151}
283 {see Dick, A Scanner, p. 182}
284 {see Dick, A Scanner, pp. 48, 50, 52}
285 {see Barthes, Barthes, p. 144}
286 {see Dick, A Scanner, pp. 265-266}

> Don't you realize how you are being exploited? How people who *control the money* are diminishing your existence to working in a fucking factory which puts black smoke up in the air, which pollutes the entire world and you are working your ass off saving money for your kids, getting pennies while they are making hundreds of Dollars? Don't you realize how you are being duped? *How they get your head fucked with?* How you get indoctrinated? How they have you conditioned?[287]

Arctor's existence is diminished to that of a 'reflex machine' in order to be part of a *dark circuit of product and effect.* His head is literally fucked with through Substance D and his *identity theft* culminates in his transformation into a *living dead.* Jameson outlines Science Fiction can show us the logic of *de*personalization in which the individual is held in our time.[288] It is argued that *A Scanner Darkly* mirrors the logic and ideology of capitalism via the detour of allegory.

The point of transition to the next chapter is the observation that Freck has problems to get it on and assumes it must be something they're adulterating the stuff with. “Some chemical.”[289]

---

287 {see Watkins, Punishment Park}

288 {see Jameson, Archaeologies, p. 348}

289 {see Dick, A Scanner, p. 14}

The Short-Timers (1979)

> There are almost no characters in this story, and almost no dramatic confrontations, because most of the people in it are so *sick* and so much the listless playthings of enormous forces. One of the main effects of war, after all, is that people are discouraged from being characters.[290]

Kurt Vonnegut's quote from *Slaughterhouse-Five* is the premise for the reading of Gustav Hasford's novel *The Short-Timers*. It is argued that there are almost no characters in *The Short-Timers* and the people in it are sick as well as the playthings of enormous forces. The following descriptions will illustrate the point. Before the protagonist Joker kills Cowboy he states he hardly knows him. Joker describes Chili Vendor and Daytona Dave as two guys who have absolutely nothing in common but nevertheless they are the best of friends. Alice carries a blue shopping bag, which contains 'foul smelling gook feet' he collects from enemy soldiers after he shot them dead.[291] But most of all, they are *dis*couraged from being characters. The structure of the novel is very important with regard to the interpretation. The three chapters of the novel are 'The Spirit of the Bayonet', 'Body Count', and 'Grunts.' The characters in the novel have no history and no future. The novel begins at a United States Marine Corps Recruit Depot and finishes somewhat towards the end of Joker's tour of duty in Vietnam. There is nothing before the recruit training and there is no end to the war. Consequently the characters have almost no history except the stereotyping which is due either to the regions they come from or to arbitrary choice. Names like Joker, Cowboy, or Gomer Pyle are substitutions and refer to the non-representational character of language. From the very beginning of the novel the reader enters a world of signs. Joker states he hardly knows Cowboy although they know each other from recruit training. Thus he signifies he only knows Cowboy's operational double. If the novel is read as an allegory then the crucial question is what kind of abstract idea is hidden behind the veil of war?

The protagonist Joker and the other men pass a sign that states: ALL HOPE ABANDON, YE WHO ENTER HERE. They have seen the sign a hundred times and they believe it.[292] The reference to Dante's *Divine Comedy* is read as a reference to allegory. The quote itself sets the mood of the novel, which is *hope-*

---

290 {see Kurt Vonnegut, Slaughterhouse-Five or The Children's Crusade (New York 1988), p. 164. [italics mine]}

291 {see Gustav Hasford, The Short-Timers (New York 1985), p. 55, 149, 178}

292 {see Hasford, The Short-Timers, p. 148}

lessness. The absence of hope is a strong connection to *Punishment Park* and *The Room*. Joker counters this *hopelessness* with his sense of irony that is a form of allegory. It is the classic mode of stating one thing and meaning another. DeMan outlines an ironic utterance exceeds the intention of the speaker and speech is thus rendered inauthentic. Awareness is impossible as absolute irony is a consciousness of madness. Repeated irony in a text means that its own *dis*continuity is advertised and reveals its *dis*connectedness.[293] Irony is Joker's signature feature and thus marks a repeated *dis*continuity of the text.

> The article I actually write is a masterpiece. It takes talent to convince people that war is a beautiful experience. Come one, come all to exotic Vietnam, the jewel of Southeast Asia, meet interesting, stimulating people of an ancient culture … and kill them. Be the first kid on your block to get a confirmed kill.[294]

The comment on his article actually sounds like an advertisement for a holiday and is quite revealing with regard to his job as a combat correspondent. The combat correspondent's motto is "FIRST TO GO, LAST TO KNOW, WE WILL DEFEND TO THE DEATH OUR RIGHT TO BE MISINFORMED."[295] Marshall McLuhan describes the final phase of the extensions of man as the electric age, the Age of Anxiety. One main aspect of the media (extensions of man) is the numbness that each extension brings about in the individual and society. "Subliminal and docile acceptance of media impact has made them *prisons without walls* for their human users."[296] The motto as well as the article represent an immense numbness on the part of Joker and his docile acceptance of this kind of media system imprisons his mind. The article is a masterpiece because he transforms a terrible experience (evil) into a beautiful experience (good). This is an important connection to *A Scanner* and the transmutation of 'evil into good in a process that lies hidden beneath the surface of reality.' The article is a myth that *dis*torts the experience and thus advertises its *lack of reality*. The irony highlights the *dis*connectedness between the real and the signs of the real.

There are two worlds, which are referred to in the novel. Alice wishes to be back in the World. Joker answers that back in the World (the absent real) is the crazy part and that this *world of shit* (signs of the real) is real. "In this world of

293 {see Tambling, Allegory, p. 132}

294 {see Hasford, The Short-Timers, p. 45}

295 {see Hasford, The Short-Timers, p. 64}

296 {see Marshall McLuhan, Understanding Media: The Extensions of Man (London 2001), pp. 2-6, 22}

shit, monsters live forever and everybody else dies."[297] The term 'monsters live forever' indicates an eternalizing mode of the *world of shit*. The phrasing *world of shit* is of importance here and has to be considered attentively. Julia Kristeva outlines the abject is a weight of meaninglessness. "On the edge of non-existence and hallucination, of a reality that, if I acknowledge it, annihilates me. There, abject and abjection are my safe-guards." Loathing of a piece of filth is a means of protection. Abjection is caused by the disturbance of identity, system, and order. "What does not respect borders, positions, rules."[298]

> Humping in the rain forest is like climbing a *stairway of shit* in an enormous *green room* constructed by ogres for the confinement of monster plants. Birth and death are *endless* processes here, with new life feeding on the decaying remains of the old.[299]

Again we are in an abstract room but in *The Short-Timers* the jungle becomes a green room. This *world of shit* does not respect any borders (it is full of decaying corpses) or rules (the only outcome of this cycle of production are confirmed kills) and it is a constant disturbance to identity (become a monster or die). An endless cycle of birth and death is a 'circular motion that is the deadest from of the universe.' The *world of shit* renders an abstract mechanism tangible. The body is situated in world that is dominated by an abject environment.

> We bomb these people, then we photograph them. My stories are paper bullets fired into the fat black heart of communism. I've fought to make the world safe for hypocrisy. We have met the enemy and he is us. War is good business – invest your son. Viet Nam means never having to say you're sorry. *Arbeit Macht Frei* -"[300]

For Hobbes, being a person is the same as being a hypocrite as the Greek word 'hypocrite' means to act. A person is somebody who personates himself or somebody or stands for an institution.[301] To act is allegorical and thus the term 'to make the world safe for hypocrisy' refers to a world of signs. The quote by Joker exemplifies what Barthes describes as bourgeois aphorisms that belong to metalanguage. They are a second-order language, which bears on objects already prepared. Their classical form is the maxim that must overlay one world, which is already made. The foundation of the bourgeois statement of fact is

---

297 {see Hasford, The Short-Timers, p. 158}

298 {see Julia Kristeva, Powers of Horror: An Essay on Abjection (New York 1982), pp. 2-4}

299 {see Hasford, The Short-Timers, p. 149}

300 {see Hasford, The Short-Timers, p. 60}

301 {see Tambling, Allegory, p. 140}

common sense, which is truth when it stops on the arbitrary order of him who speaks it.[302] 'We have met the enemy and he is us' is derived from a famous comic strip, 'War is good business – invest your son' is from an anti-war campaign, 'Viet Nam means *never* having to say you're sorry' is an allusion to the popular line 'Love means never having to say you're sorry' from the film *Love Story* (Arthur Hiller, 1970). The most notorious quote *Arbeit Macht Frei* is a reference to the Third Reich and in particular to the death camps. Joker also described Parris Island as a suburban death camp.[303] All these statements are supposed to overlay a world already made and a statement of fact like 'war is good business' or a word like *never* give the appearance of fact and eternity. *Arbeit Macht Frei* is the best example for substitution as it illustrates the gap between words and meaning. *Arbeit Macht Frei* epitomizes that language is non-representational. This quote is Joker's imitation of bourgeois aphorisms and through his irony becomes a mirror that reflects bourgeois metalanguage.

"War is ugly because the truth can be ugly and war is very sincere."[304] War is read as a metaphor that makes a certain mechanism visible. Foucault outlines that Marx on several occasions stressed the analogy between the *division of labor* and those of *military tactics*. Discipline is an art of distributing bodies and of composing forces in order to obtain an efficient machine. The soldier is above all a fragment of a mobile space, of a multi-segmentary machine and thus the body is reduced to its functionality. *Combinatory* is another important characteristic of an individuality that is created by discipline out of the control over the body. It means the composition of forces.[305] The metaphor of war makes an important aspect of the composition of forces visible. Joker comments on the statement of a Colonel that war is serious business. He jokes that war is a serious business and this (he points to a wasted NVA hanging in the wire) is our *gross* national product.[306] The analogy between war and capitalism is at the core of the novel. The product of war is death, which makes it the gross national product. He employs the double meaning of gross / *gross* in order to emphasize the *gross* nature of an economy whose sole product is death which is reminiscent of Mors ontologica. An efficient machine (economy) depends on the composition of forces and in *The Short-Timers* a very particular characteristic of individuality is

---

302 {see Barthes, Selected, pp. 144-145}

303 {see Hasford, The Short-Timers, p. 3}

304 {see Hasford, The Short-Timers, pp. 175-176}

305 {see Foucault, Discipline, pp. 163-164, 167}

306 {see Hasford, The Short-Timers, p. 83}

created in order to optimize the machine. Althusser outlines the ambiguity of the term subject lies in the fact that the individual is interpellated as a (free) subject so that he shall submit freely to the commandments of the Subject. The subject shall make the gestures and actions of his subjection all by himself.[307] Arctor and Joker both face the same dilemma as both are forced to make a decision by themselves. Both novels illustrate the necessity to make the gestures of subjection all by oneself. In *A Scanner* Arctor's indoctrination is to follow as the next quote illustrates. "Well, following the least line of resistance, that's the rule of survival. Following, not leading."[308] Power produces the *living dead* in order to achieve limitless subjection. In *The Short-Timers* Joker's conditioning aims at leading. "Nobody *wants* to lead, maggot, but somebody *has* to."[309] The crucial difference lies in the word 'survival' as the metaphor of war as business does not include survival. Sergeant Gerheim marks the point in saying that Marines die because that is what they are there for but the Marine Corps will live *forever*.[310] 'Marines die because that is what they are there for' expresses the utmost degree of the reduction of the body to functionality. Sergeant Gerheim's language is the language of the oppressor and aims a eternalizing with the statement that the Marine Corps will live *forever*.

Joker states that maybe the Crotch can fuck him but he won't spread his own cheeks. He does not see himself as the author of this farce and emphasizes he is just acting out his role. He is a corporal and does not send anybody out to get blown away.[311] Arctor and Joker both are actors in a *game of power* who act out their roles. The metaphor that the Crotch can fuck Joker but he won't spread his cheeks is reminiscent of the realm of the anal in *The Room*. Again a *space of metaphor* is encountered where a sacrifice is demanded. Lacan positions man as a moral being in the realm of the anal and ranks foremost the materialist in this realm. In this case the notion of morality requires the inclusion of the forms of subjectivation. The ultimate sacrifice is to make the gesture of subjection all by oneself, i.e. to spread one's own cheeks. The quote also demonstrates how a mode of domination seeks to exert power via sexuality first over the body and secondly over the mind. During the whole novel Joker repeatedly refuses to lead which is a crucial aspect with regard to functionality as well as the composition

307 {see Althusser, On Ideology, p. 56}

308 {see Dick, A Scanner, p. 244}

309 {see Hasford, The Short-Timers, p. 9}

310 {see Hasford, The Short-Timers, p. 9}

311 {see Hasford, The Short-Timers, p. 161}

of forces. He argues that he writes anything like war cures cancer or war is fun to eat but he does not kill. Grunts kill but he only watches. After Cowboy's death he has no other option than to become the new sergeant. “Semper Fi, Mom and Dad, Semper Fi, my werewolf children.” The motto of the Marine Corps is Semper Fidelis, which means “*Always* Faithful.”[312] With this vow Joker submits freely to the commandments of the Subject. The whole novel leads to this pivotal point that marks absolute control over the body and the mind.

The term werewolf establishes a connection to Marx's definition of the capitalist as werewolf whose hunger drives him to replace 'living labor' with 'dead labor.'[313] Sergeant Gerheim looks to Joker like a werewolf who is baring his fangs. The marines at Parris Island are described as a hundred young werewolves with guns in their hands. Joker is afraid a poge colonel might bite him in the neck and when he grins he bares his vampire fangs. “Poges try to kill you on the inside. Poges leave your body intact because your muscles are all they want from you anyway.”[314] This argument pursues the idea that the comparison between werewolves and Marine Corps stands as a metaphor for the capitalist. The vampire is like the werewolf another Gothic creature whose aim is to substitute living labor with dead labor. Focus is laid on the inside as the outside must remain intact and internal relationships bring us back to the forms of subjectivation. Throughout the novel Joker's superiors are offended by a peace symbol that he wears. The vampire colonel asks him to *confess* that he wants peace. Joker asks the colonel if that is not what the colonel wants and does not get an answer. But the colonel says later: “Someday, Corporal, when you're a little older, you'll realize how naive -” The poge colonel's voice breaks on “naive.”[315] The peace symbol is a vital point of intersection with *The Last House on the Left*. It functions as another instance of control over the mind. The symbol describes things as natural and thus is read as a bourgeois myth that *dis*torts signification. The reference to naivety hints at the deceptive side of the symbol. Barthes's advice is to focus on the thing that has been distorted. *The meaning of the word peace has been alienated by the concept of war.* The metaphor of the Marine as capitalist is read as bourgeois ex-nomination. Barthes states bourgeois ex-nomination characterizes at once bourgeois ideology and myth itself. The bourgeoisie hides the

312 {see Hasford, The Short-Timers, pp. 60, 18, 179}

313 {see Gelder, The Horror, p. 285}

314 {see Hasford, The Short-Timers, p. 161}

315 {see Hasford, The Short-Timers, pp. 137-139}

fact that it is the bourgeoisie and thereby produces myth.[316] Allegory as an enactment of abstract concepts mirrors bourgeois ex-nomination via the *dis*placement of language. Discipline individualizes bodies by a location that does not give them a fixed position. Discipline distributes bodies and circulates them in a *network of relations*.[317] The metaphor of the Marine Corps renders the network of relations tangible and illustrates the distribution of bodies.

Brian Massumi outlines the turn to affect is about opening the body to the indeterminacy of autonomic responses. Affect refers to an openness of a body and the temporality of affect can be described as thresholds, bifurcation, and emergence. The link between the subject and technology is bodily affectivity itself. Technology enters the human subject first and foremost through the body. The affective capacity of the body enables us to recognize this.[318] *The body-object relation is an essential part of control.* Foucault outlines the relations of the body with the object it manipulates are precisely defined by discipline. The instrumental coding of the body consists of a breakdown of a total gesture into two series. One includes the parts of the body to be used and one includes parts of the object manipulated. These two series are combined and the ultimate aim of this 'manœuvre' is to introduce power. Thus a body-machine complex is created and a synthesis is established whose aim is to *link the product to the apparatus of production. Organic* is the last characteristic of an individuality which is created by discipline out of the control over the body and describes the coding of activities. [319] The mechanical centaur is a metaphor for the *body-object relation.* Joker describes the tank driver's face as coated with a thin film of oil and sweat. He sweats oil to lubricate the tank. Iron has entered into his soul and he has become a component of the tank. The tank driver became a mechanical centaur, half man, half tank.[320] The mechanical centaur is an example of the marriage between body and technology. This synthesis also exemplifies the reduction of the body to functionality (sweat serves as lubrication for the tank). The novel places special focus on the subject and how he transforms his own mode of being.

---

316 {see Barthes, Selected, p. 135}

317 {see Foucault, Discipline, p. 146}

318 {see Melissa Gregg and Gregory J. Seigworth, The Affect Theory Reader (Durham 2010), pp. 209-210, 212}

319 {see Foucault, Discipline, pp. 152-153, 167 }

320 {see Hasford, The Short-Timers, pp. 79, 111}

The songs the recruits have to sing during military training is another aspect of bourgeois maxims and illustrates the coding of activities. “This is my rifle, this is my gun; one is for fighting and one is for fun. And: I don't want no teen-aged queen; all I want is my M-14.” Sergeant Gerheim reinforces their song with the assertion that their rifle is the only pussy they will get. They are married to their weapon and they *will* be faithful.[321] The body-machine complex is created with a marriage between body and rifle. Docility and utility are the ultimate aim of this strategy. Sexuality serves as the central point of support for this strategy which invades first the body and secondly the mind. Sexuality is substituted by technology in order to *penetrate* the body with the aim of total control. “The worker puts his life into the object and this means that it no longer belongs to him but to the object.”[322] The loss of Joker's life is illustrated by the name he gives his rifle, Vanessa. When he thinks about his girlfriend Vanessa back home he fantasizes about her thighs, her dark nipples, her full lips. But these images do not give him a hard-on anymore. “I guess it must be the saltpeter in our food, like they say.”[323] This almost sounds exactly like Freck. Both have lost their taste in sexual relations and assume they are poisoned. A *world of murk / shit* (a world of signs) has opened up for them and this *world of murk / shit* is focused on the *body-object relation*. This relation results in Mors ontologica, the death of the spirit, identity, and the essential nature. Joker sees how blood pours out of the barrel of his rifle and flows up onto his hands. The blood moves and breaks up into living fragments. Each fragment is a spider and millions of tiny red spiders of blood crawl up his arms, across his face and into his mouth.[324] The figure of the spider is of central importance as it is not only a metaphor for his fragmentation. In Native American mythology Iktomi is an ancient trickster who is also called 'Spider.' As with other tricksters, Iktomi deceives others for his own gain. The character of the trickster is a complex blend of personalities and he is frequently seen as a creator or re-creator of the world.[325] The *body-object relation* in the first chapter 'The Spirit of the Bayonet' finds its conclusion in the spider invasion. Joker's body is literally *penetrated* by these agents of fragmentation. They also are supposed to accommodate Joker to a *world of shit* in order

321 {see Hasford, The Short-Timers, pp. 12-13}

322 {see Marx, Selected, p. 79}

323 {see Hasford, The Short-Timers, p. 27}

324 {see Hasford, The Short-Timers, p. 32}

325 {see Dawn E. Bastian; Judy K. Mitchell, Handbook of Native American Mythology (Oxford 2008), pp. 177, 210}

increase domination over his body. *This world of shit is a web of deception that aims solely at the increase of production.*

McLuhan points out the effects of technology do not occur at the level of opinions or concepts, but alter patterns of perception. He describes the serious artist as an expert who is aware of the changes in sense perception.[326] Joker perceives the jungle (the green room) as their *real enemy.* Everything there is samey-same: the trees, vines like dead snakes, leafy plants. The monotony and sameness leaves Joker and the others unmoored.[327] Kucukalic points out that Arctor is rueful about the chain of commerce and the commerce of chains that produce a culture of sameness, unoriginality, and meaninglessness.[328] The link between *The Short-Timers* and *A Scanner* is the perception of an American culture of sameness. The jungle as the *real enemy* embodies an environment that is monotone and unchanging. The noun *enemy* implies hostility and the verb unmoored implies a loss of reality.

Another peculiar aspect of Joker's perception is the creation of a blend between the human world and the world of things: Rafter Man hugs his black-body Nikons like metal babies; legs are machines winding you up like a mechanical toy; an exploded gunship is a gutted carcass of aluminium and plexiglass; intestines are black rope; a tank is a like a big iron dragon, choppers are monster grasshoppers.[329] Hasford is an expert in observing the alteration of perception in American society during the seventies. Joker's complete sense of perception is dominated by the combination between bodies and objects. Karl Marx outlines the worker becomes a commodity that is the cheaper the more commodities he creates and thus the depreciation of the human world (opportunities of living) progresses in direct proportion to the increase in value of the world of things (means of living). *In political economy the objectification of labor appears as a loss of reality for the worker.*[330] Joker's perception is altered due to the objectification of labor. The progress of the deprecation of the human world is illustrated by the *gross* business goal of war, which is death. The increase in value of the world of things is the creation of more commodities, which are confirmed kills. In the second chapter 'Body Count' Joker has a dope dream of death in which he feels himself breaking up into to three pieces: body, mind and spirit. The mind

326 {see McLuhan, Understanding, p. 19}

327 {see Hasford, The Short-Timers, pp. 150-151 }

328 {see Kucukalic, Philip K. Dick, p. 126}

329 {see Hasford, The Short-Timers, pp. 48-49, 77, 100, 125, 129, 148}

330 {see Marx, Selected, p. 78}

explains to the body that *they* play this *game* and that interference is not allowed. The mind concludes losing men seems to be the whole point of the *game*. Spirit refuses to return with body and mind. The body convinces the mind that they do not need the spirit.[331] It has to be noted that so far every work under discussion employed the metaphor of the game. The dope dream of death is a visual depiction of Joker's inner fragmentation. The *game of power* in *The Short-Timers* is invested in the production of death as the whole point of the game is losing men. Marx states that the more values the worker creates the more valueless and worthless he becomes, the more powerful the work the more powerless the worker.[332] Joker marvels at that ultimate power of death. He realizes that his own weapon is capable of doing this dark magic thing to any human being.[333] The term 'dark magic thing' is read as the reversal of a magic trick. Joker and his weapon create nothing out of something. The 'ultimate power of death' illustrates the power of Joker's work and thus his own powerlessness.

The last focal point of this chapter is refraction, which is an instrument of contemporary capitalism and its centralizing political vocation. Barot outlines one aspect of the omnipotence of the *Monoform* is that it is unthinkable to imagine the public could take any other part in television than via game shows or reality shows. The *Monoform* is repetitive, foreseeable and closed to any participation of the spectators. It is an extremely controlled space, which treats the spectator as immature and thus the spectator is in need of familial presentations in order to be manipulated. The *Monoform* has the power to modify our *perception of time* that is a key instrument in the regulation of the public. Monoform productions are a *reification of time,* which mirrors the power of the *Monoform* to bring us to lose any sense of history or social bonding. In order to reclaim a sense of history one must render the monoformation evadable and political. Barot emphasizes the importance of a struggle against the material and intellectual reification via contributing to the recapture of a *political meaning,* which is the space that embodies the vital contradiction between the real and the possible.[334] Joker states that almost every Marine carries a short-timer's calendar of his tour of duty. The designs of 'The Short-Timer' may vary but most tend to utilize a big-busted woman-child cut up into pieces like a puzzle. "Each day another fragment of her delicious anatomy is inked out. Her crotch being reserved, of

331 {see Hasford, The Short-Timers, p. 104}

332 {see Karl Marx, Selected Writings (Oxford 1977), p. 79}

333 {see Hasford, The Short-Timers, p. 130}

334 {see Barot, Camera, pp.91-93}

course, for those last few days in country."[335] The 'glorious rotation dates circled in red' on the Short-Timers may be different but they have the same significance which is *Home*. Towards the end of the novel Joker notes that for those who survive home won't be there anymore and they won't be there anymore. "Upon each of our brains the war has lodged itself, a black crab feeding."[336] War and junk are both compared to parasites inside the human body. The sickness of the protagonist in *The Room* was also read a huge internal parasite with the sole aim to prevent man from inventing himself. This argument pursues the idea that the title of the novel is the key to the ideology critique hidden behind the veil of war. The calendar is a metaphor for the *Monoform* whose aim as part of the ISAs is the reproduction of the relations of production. The Marine Corps (Semper Fi, my werewolf children) represents the familial presentation that manipulates. *The Short-Timers* is a hallucinatory space that serves as a mirror to ideology. *The tour of duty is emblematic for the reification of time that entails the loss of any sense of history and social bonding.* The *world of shit* reveals the loss of all values and the loss of *Home* leads to the ultimate loss of identity.

The point of transition to the last chapter is a quote from Joker: "Nobody asks us why we're smiling because nobody wants to know. The ugly that civilians see in war focuses on spilled guts. To see human beings clearly, that is ugly. To carry death in your smile, that is ugly."[337]

335 {see Hasford, The Short-Timers, p. 45}

336 {see Hasford, The Short-Timers, pp. 154, 176}

337 {see Hasford, The Short-Timers, p. 175}

Dawn of the Dead (1979)

> You are hypnotized by this place, all of you. It's so bright and neatly wrapped you don't see that it's a *prison*, too.[338]

This argument started with a horror film and it finishes with a horror film. The horror genre is able to approach social and historical issues because the genre classification obscures the content. *The Last House* illustrates the collapse of society whereas *Dawn of the Dead* (George A. Romero, 1979) moves the setting beyond the collapse of society. George A. Romero's inspiration for the zombie trilogy was spawned by Richard Matheson's novel *I am Legend.* Romero describes his project as an allegory about the issues implicated by an incoming revolutionary society replacing an existing social order.[339] Romero's reference to allegory is in tune with the allegorical approach of this argument. As *I am Legend* was his inspiration the novel will be included in order to illustrate some vital points. Cook states Romero started out as an auteur in the original French sense that designates a writer-director who shapes his material from script through post-production. Romero did that in the under-financed netherworld of low-end exploitation films and his film *Night of the Living Dead* is regarded as a watershed of modern horror. Cook outlines there are elements of social satire in the film's sequel *Dawn of the Dead,* which is set mostly in a shopping mall. He compares the attack of the zombies on humans and their mindless materialistic rampage as the moral equivalent of shopping.[340] Critics as well as fans hailed it as a masterpiece of horror that came to epitomize America in the seventies with the shopping mall setting and zombie 'consumers.'[341] According to Barot, the horror film genre is a sub-genre of social-political films and establishes *counter*utopias. These dystopias are a *dis*solution of the social state and unsettle the certainties of a world regulated by laws. Hence the fragility of these laws is exposed.[342] This argument focuses on humans and not on zombies as the *dis*solution of the social state becomes apparent in the human experience of this *counter*utopia. The prefix counter- implicates a substitution, which establishes a con-

---

338 {see George A. Romero, Dawn of the Dead (USA 1979)}

339 {see Paul R. Gagne, The Zombies that ate Pittsburgh: The Films of George A. Romero (New York 1987), p. 24}

340 {see Cook, Lost, pp. 229-230, 232}

341 {see Gagne, The Zombies, p. 83}

342 {see Barot, Camera, p. 34}

nection to the impossibility of keeping an abstract concept abstract. The abstract concept encountered here is the struggle between a majority and a minority.

According to Benjamin, allegory corresponds to a perception of the *world in ruins*. He concludes allegory is therefore the *art of the fragment*.[343] Francine, the female lead character, wakes up from a nightmare in the opening scene of *Dawn* but is she really awake or is she still dreaming? Tambling states the dream gives freedom to the writers of allegory. Dreams have a fluidity that yields a special form of allegory.[344] The collapse of society that unfolds has a nightmarish quality as the audience encounters a *world in ruins*. Critics mostly disregard the beginning of the film but within the range of this argument it is considered to be very important. Francine and her boyfriend Stephen work for a television station. Roger and Peter work for the police force. The television networks as well as the police system are breaking down and all four ask themselves if it is right to abandon their posts. Baudrillard states "information and security, in all their forms, instead of intensifying or creating the "social relation," are on the contrary entropic processes, modalities of the end of the social."[345] In the scenario of *Dawn* information (television) and security (police) are indeed entropic processes. The protagonists, especially the police officers, recognize the modalities of the end of the social and regard escape as the only solution. Robert Neville, the protagonist from *I Am Legend* states morality had fallen with society and that he is his own ethic now.[346] This quote corresponds to Peter's statement that they are thieves and they are bad guys.[347] The collapse of society has created a space devoid of morality and Peter is well aware of that. Gregory A. Waller outlines *Dawn* refuses to present the audience with situations in which moral or political distinctions are perfectly clear.[348] This argument pursues the idea that Romero goes as far as to abolish any Manichean distinctions. Romero presents the audience with binary distinctions only to *dis*integrate them into thin air. Baudrillard states the ideal form of simulation is the collapse of poles.[349] Romero creates a an allegorical space that is beyond equivalences and Manichean aesthetics.

According to Waller, *Dawn* is among the most noteworthy examinations of the role and the representation of violence in American culture. He refers to the

343 {see Tambling, Allegory, p. 110}
344 {see Tambling, Allegory, p. 7}
345 {see Baudrillard, In the Shadow, p. 51}
346 {see Matheson. I Am Legend, p. 54}
347 {see Romero, Dawn of the Dead}
348 {see Gelder, The Horror, p. 263}
349 {see Baudrillard, In the Shadow, p. 48}

contention that modern horror became what is called 'hard-core' pornography of violence by the virtual elimination of censorship. The equation of explicitly violent horror with pornographic gore is often based on the assumption that truly effective horror is indirect and suggestive, leaving the horrific primarily to the viewer's imagination. He further outlines the most important criticism of modern horror's so called pornography of violence was directed more explicitly toward ideological rather than stylistic questions.[350] This argument also pursues the idea that *pornographic violence* addresses ideological issues. On their escape the small group stops at a shopping mall and because they find everything they desire at the mall they *annex* the place. They kill the zombies and clean the place of the bodies. They barricade it up against intruders and enjoy the place in an excessive shopping orgy. They are like Neville who describes himself as a weird Robinson Crusoe who is imprisoned on an island of night and surrounded by oceans of death.[351] The island in *Dawn* is an island of pleasure that is supposed to reconcile them with the fact that the *world is in ruins*.

Francine states they are hypnotized by the place and that they are also prisoners. Allegorical prison-existence is encountered in order to depict a particular life style in American society. A viral disease causes the collapse of society. Foucault describes a plague-stricken town as a *frozen space* in which each individual is fixed in his place. The plague as a form of disorder calls for multiple separations and an organization in depth of surveillance and control. *This leads to an intensification and ramification of power.* All authorities that exercise individual control function according to binary division.[352] The initial binary division is between humans and zombies but during the course of the film Peter realizes that 'they are us.' Again the audience has to face the collapse of poles. The control of the place demands an *intensification of power,* which is illustrated by violence that is exerted in a business like manner due to the binary division. Roger addresses a zombie with the words: “Hey Ugly.” This is one central point of intersection with the violence in *The Short-Timers*. “The ugly that civilians see in war focuses on spilled guts. To see human beings clearly, that is ugly. To carry death in your smile, that is ugly.” The following frame illustrates that Roger actually smiles while he is about to shoot a zombie. Romero focuses not on the ugliness of carnage but on the ugliness of a smile that carries death. To carry death in your smile is *pornographic violence*.

---

350 {see Gelder, The Horror, p. 260-261}

351 {see Richard Matheson, I Am Legend (London 1999), p. 77}

352 {see Foucault, Discipline, pp. 195-199}

Figure 7: Dawn of the Dead © "To carry death in your smile, that is ugly."

The scene when Peter and Roger find a weapon store named *Gunner's Den* in the mall is accompanied by music that sounds tribal which implies that not only the zombies are driven by their pure, motorized instincts. Baudrillard compares the American society to a primitive society with regard to conformity. In a primitive society it would be absurd to distinguish oneself morally through *diso*-bedience of a collective ritual. This kind of conformity is the result of a morality that demands an immediate adherence to a set of rules.[353] The *Gunner's Den* is a symbol for the adherence to a moral set of rules that dictates the use and acceptance of violence as a life style. The power of symbolism is a means of control for ideology and the issue of morals addresses here the internal relationship, the forms of subjectivation. "We have *enslaved ourselves,* by our own petty, circumscribed view of life."[354] This observation by Henry Miller is of central importance for the interpretation of *Dawn* and particular emphasis is placed on the expression *enslaved ourselves*. Romero states he desired to reflect the seventies and the mall as a temple of the materialistic 'me' generation provided the perfect vehicle. Actress Gaylen Ross notes the symbols have lost their meaning due to a lack of context. The protagonists in the film give those symbols meaning only to

353 {see Baudrillard, Amérique, p. 91}

354 {see Miller, The Colossus, p. 86. [italics mine]}

realize that none of it is valuable anymore.[355] It is argued that the lacking context illustrates these symbols never did have any value apart from the context. Ideology aims at the misrepresentation of the world to ourselves and after the collapse of society they realize the effect of ideology is *dis*tortion. The mall signifies their entrapment in a world without referentiality. The mall embodies the 'logic of the capitalist centralization of value.'[356] The terminology employed with regard to the mall derives from a bourgeois background: the mall is a 'goldmine' and the keys to the shops are 'keys to the kingdom.' This terminology illustrates the gaps between words and meaning, it illustrates signification apart from content. The strategy of a continual *dis*placement of language is supposed to mirror the ruling ideology.

The terminology establishes a network of signification and reveals that people are manipulated to desire to gain access to the kingdom. Peter asks Roger if he is *game* before they explore the mall. The conquest of the mall is another expression of the *game of power,* as they want the kingdom all to themselves. After they reach the security of a shop Roger wants to know how they are going to get back and Peter answers: "Who the hell cares, let's go shopping first." After weeks of indulging in the luxury of the mall and ignoring the collapse of society Francine states: "What have we done to ourselves."[357] This statement refers to the self-destructive quality of their behavior. For Henry Miller, all department stores are symbols of sickness and emptiness. *They symbolize an obscure and incurable malady.*[358] The mall is literally deserted after they *annexed* it. Not only the zombies symbolize *an obscure and incurable malady* but also the mall represents this kind of *malady*. The themes of the mall and malady represent an important connection to *A Scanner*.

> Ahead, one of those giant shopping malls surrounded by a wall that you bounced off like a rubber ball – unless you had a credit card on you and passed in through the electronic hoop. [...] Lots of people moved on in through the gate, but he figured many were no doubt window-shopping. Not all that many people can have the bread or the urge to buy this time of day, he reflected. It's early, just past two. At night; that was when. The shops all lit up. He could- all the brothers and sister could- see the lights from without, like showers of sparks, like a *fun park* for grown-up kids.[359]

355 {see Gagne, The Zombies, pp. 87, 89}
356 {see Baudrillard, Simulacra, p. 11}
357 {see Romero, Dawn of the Dead}
358 {see Miller, The Obelisk, p. 255}
359 {see Dick, A Scanner, pp.10-11. [italics mine]}

Freck's description of the mall also applies to the mall in *Dawn*. There are several scenes that show the four protagonists playing video games or different kinds of sports. The mall is a fun park for grown-up kids and offers them the possibility to forget about the collapse of society, to endure the unendurable. The three works explored with regard to the late seventies share one vital common thread. Dick, Hasford, and Romero all explore the forms of subjectivation, an internal relationship with the self that leads to the transformation of the own mode of being.

Barot states, every image in a film captures and mediates parts of a social reality. Cinema is a direct or indirect statement of the common world. Films with focus on social critic depict different kinds of discrimination, difficulties with power, possible sources of alienation and how they affect social life.[360] The following image is an indirect statement on American society and its abstract quality is enormous. Francine is posing in front of a mirror and the audience sees this *dis*torted image of a society that is violent and grotesque. This allegorical image defines violence and materiality as a source of alienation and illustrates the insane impact on social life.

Figure 8: Dawn of the Dead © This image shows a body in its violent and violating dimension

360 {see Barot, Camera, pp. 27, 32}

Stam suggests two points are vital for the explanation of the public's attraction to a text or a medium. First, one must sort out ideological effects that manipulate people into complicity with existing social relations. Second, one must focus on the kernel of utopian fantasy and thus reach beyond social relations. The medium is regarded as a projected fulfillment of what is desired as well as absent within the status quo. It is important to realize the distorted undertones of utopia in mass media and to point out the real obstacles, which make utopia less realizable. According to Stam, the American mass media capitalize on the frustrated desire for an egalitarian society.[361] The ideological effects in *Dawn* are identified as primitive conformity and an excessive indulgence in pleasure. Those effects manipulate the people into complicity with existing social relations. The mall is a metaphor for the desire of equality but the distorted undertones of this material dream world are mere homogenization.

> Pleasure (whether perverse or not) was always mediated by a technical apparatus, by a mechanism of real objects but more often of phantasms – it always implies an intermediary manipulation of scenes or gadgets. Here, pleasure is only orgasm, that is to say, confused on the same wave length with the violence of the technical apparatus, and homogenized by the only technique, one summed up by a single object: the automobile.[362]

In *Dawn* pleasure is shopping and the place that sums up the technique is the mall. The utopian fantasy of equality veils the goal of the ruling ideology to achieve homogeneity. Ideology is a pure illusion whose reality is external to it and thus the act of shopping gives ideology material existence. Actually, the mall is an agent of delusion and represents a system of exclusion, as a customer without money is a persona non grata. Money is the god of this universe but after the collapse of society its lacking referentiality is revealed. Priest points out that magic is an illusion, a temporary suspension of reality.[363] The notion of a *temporary suspension of reality* bears an interesting resemblance to Althusser's notion of an *ignorance of reality*. In *Dawn* the illusion is what Althusser terms an *ignorance of reality* which is solely invested in the reproduction of the relations of exploitation.[364] Francine states the mall hypnotizes them and that they do not see that it is a prison, too. The term 'hypnotized' is read as a reference to an *ignorance of reality* and the metaphor of the prison relates to their exploita-

361 {see Stam, Film, pp. 310, 312, 314}

362 {see Baudrillard, Simulacra, p. 116}

363 {see Priest, The Prestige, p. 219}

364 {see Althusser, On Ideology, pp. 56-57}

tion. "After all, an illusion, no matter how convincing, remained nothing more than an illusion. At least objectively. But subjectively – quite the opposite entirely."[365] Dick illustrates here the crucial point because an objective point of view is exactly the problem. In *Dawn*, a scientist on a television debate underlines the importance to remain rational and logical. The television host counters that scientists always think in this kind of terms but that is not how people really are.[366] *The conclusion is that people are subjective and exactly this trait renders the illusion so powerful.* The ruthless exploitation of this trait is a constant source of alienation and thus the *world in ruins* portrayed in *Dawn* depicts the loss of all values.

Baudrillard describes the coup de théâtre démocratique as democracy, which demands that all of its citizens begin the race even whereas egalitarianism insists that they all finish even.[367] The disease is read as a metaphor for egalitarianism as all citizens finish the race even without exception. In *I am Legend* there was no union among the infected and their need was their only motivation.[368] Romero changed this aspect as the zombies are no cannibals, they do not prey on each other but only on warm flesh. Their need for food is still their only motivation but they form a union against mankind who is fragmented and *dis*jointed. The raiders at the end of the film start a war with the survivors in the mall and cause deaths on both sides. According to Henry Miller, the great fundamental lack is the total absence of anything approaching a communal existence.[369] The absence of a communal existence is apparent in *Dawn* as there is no union among each other and hence the zombies become the new majority who reclaims eventually the mall.

The last aspect of *Dawn* under discussion is filmic reflexivity. The Brechtian aesthetic of importance here is the *transformation of production relations*. This describes the critique of the system in general and the apparatuses that produce and distribute culture.[370] Romero as an auteur is well aware of the 'commerce of auteurism' in the late seventies. "In the late 1960s and early 1970s, auteurism became much more to the American cinema than simply a mode of aesthetic discourse." Cook further argues there was a brief reign of creative power

365 {see Philip K. Dick, Minority Report (London 2002), p. 269}

366 {see Romero, Dawn of the Dead}

367 {see Baudrillard, Amérique, p. 92}

368 {see Matheson, I Am Legend, p. 17}

369 {see Miller, The Colossus, p. 125}

370 {see Stam, Film, pp. 146, 156-157}

of a rising generation of independent filmmakers. But finally the world's most capital-intensive production context put an end to the European ideal of authorship by the end of the decade. “I make films for audiences, not critics. It is a business, I'm not dumb” (Debra Hill, line producer of the Halloween series). Auteurism was turned into a mere marketing tool and the cinema of rebellion was replaced by impersonal and corporate cinema.[371] Ideology critique in *Dawn* is also read as a critique of the contemporary film industry and the selling out of auteurism towards the end of the decade. Stam outlines reflexivity is symptomatic of a methodological self-consciousness and its tendency to scrutinize its own instruments. Filmic reflexivity refers in a broad sense to the process by which films foreground their own production, their authorship, their textual procedures, their intertextual influences, or their reception. Film theory during the seventies was influenced by Althusser as well as Brecht and thus came to deem reflexivity as a political obligation.[372] For example the act of shopping can be substituted with the act of going to the cinema and thus *Dawn* foregrounds the reception of the film. Romero is able to combine the political obligation with the social and historical issues he addresses as the rise of corporate cinema coincided with the rise of consumption. Auteur cinema like *Dawn* is invested in an active engagement with social relations and change whereas corporate cinema aims at a passive experience and misrecognition of social relations.

371 {see Cook, Lost, pp. 156, 238}

372 {see Stam, Film, p. 151}

Jetons Bas ce Vieux Plâtrage qui Masque la Façade de l'Art! or Real Innovations Attack the Base

> *Things are the way they are.* That is horrible, the perpetual torment ... And to think that one has only to do oneself in – and the riddle is solved! But *is* that a solution? Is it not slightly ridiculous? Moral suicide is so much easier. Adjusting to life, as they say. Not to what should be or ought be.[373]

«Le génie est nécessairement inégal. Il n'est pas de hautes montagnes sans profonds précipices.»[374] The works within the range of this argument explore the 'profonds précipices' or the dark spaces of the American experience in the seventies. But the very existence of dark spaces implies the possibility of hautes montagnes. The artists recapture *political meaning* and create allegorical spaces, which embody a vital connection between the real and the possible. The abstract idea behind their works of art makes them important: America. They portray inherent problems in American society and search for an inaccessible truth. *Things are the way they are.* Miller realized that the statement of fact is a principal figure of bourgeois myths and rebelled against it. The artists under discussion have explored 'moral suicide' and 'adjusting to life' in different variations. The conclusion is that there is no morality but only a moral superstructure. Miller states the superstructure is a lie and the foundation a huge quaking fear.[375] Brecht recommends that real innovations attack the *base.*[376] Althusser outlines the spatial metaphor of the edifice reveals that the *base* in the last instance determines the whole edifice. The economic *base* is the unity of productive forces and the relations of production.[377] Craven, Watkins, Selby, Dick, Hasford and Romero are all dedicated to expose the relations of productions that are relations of exploitation. They attack the *base* and create a *prestige de réalité.*

The allegorical image from the film *THX-1138* (George Lucas, 1971) comprises the whole range of this argument. The first section of this argument reveals a focus on brutal authority and the tolerance of sadistic violence (Kent State, My Lai) whereas the second section illustrates a focus on bodies and tech-

373 {see Henry Miller, The World of Sex (New York 1965), p. 40}

374 {see Hugo, Cromwell, p. 107. "The texture of character is inevitably uneven. There is no high mountain without a deep abyss." [trans. mine]}

375 {see Miller, The Obelisk, p. 120}

376 {see Brecht, Mahagonny, p. 73}

377 {see Althusser, On Ideology, pp. 8-10}

nology (materialistic 'me' generation). *THX-1138* reflects the zeitgeist of the early seventies and also anticipated the road society would take towards the late seventies. The particular constellation of the different works within the range of this discussion and the arrangement of mobile parts offers a certain meaning. The common thread is the kind of reality that is produced by power.

Figure 9: THX 1138 © This image connects the themes of a relation with authority and a relation with technology

> The reality in question in this mechanism (the mirror recognition of the Subject and of the individuals interpellated as subjects), the reality which is necessarily ignored (méconnue) in the very forms of recognition (ideology = misrecognition / ignorance) is indeed, in the last resort, the reproduction of the relations of production and of the relations deriving from them.[378]

Priest outlines that magic *always* improves.[379] In this context magic is read as a substitution for ideology and 'always' indicates a language that aims at eternalizing. The improvement focuses on the ignorance of reality, which is the point that is attacked by the artists within the range of this argument. It does not matter if it is authority or technology as both produce the same reality that is characterized by *inhumanity* and *inequality*. "And as long as human beings can sit and watch with hands folded while their fellow-men are tortured and butchered so long will civilization be a hollow mockery, a wordy phantom suspended like a mirage above a swelling sea of murdered carcases."[380] The artists are kindred spirits

378 {see Althusser, On Ideology, pp. 56-57}

379 {see Priest, The Prestige, p. 283}

380 {see Miller, The Colossus, p. 177}

with Miller and depict America as a hollow mockery and a wordy phantom. *Inhumanity* and *inequality* in American society as a way things are is the most unbearable realization for them and the most unacceptable.

Foucault describes a new technology of power, which is not disciplinary. This mode of power does utilize, integrate, and modify disciplinary technology. Discipline addresses man-as-body whereas biopower addresses man-as-species. Man-as-species is regularized and the power of regularization consists in making live and letting die. Sexuality is a matter for discipline as well as for regularization because it exists at the point where body and population meet. Biopower has disciplinary as well as regulatory effects. The play of technologies (discipline and regulation) succeeds in covering the whole surface that lies between body and population. The emergence of biopower inscribes the *function of death* in the mechanism of the State. Foucault describes racism as the break between what must live and what must die. The power of normalization must become racist if it wishes to exercise the right to kill which includes every form of indirect murder. The most murderous States are also the most racist.[381] The break between what must live and what must die is sadly present in all the analyzed works: Krug as embodiment of institutionalized violence, the murderous politics of Punishment Park, the sadistic and violent destruction of Mrs. Haagstromm, Arctor's transformation into a *living dead,* the Marine who is supposed to die and whose task is to kill, and the killing of zombies. Murder and mayhem are at the core of those works in order to reveal the murderous and racist nature of the State. Different kinds of disciplinary techniques have been encountered with the sole aim to produce docile and utile bodies. These bodies have in common that they are situated in a world of signs where everything has been replaced with its operational double. "In fact, the only real anarchism is that of power."[382] The *game of power* exemplifies that winning is only possible with trickery and thus reveals the deceptive nature of the game. All the works within the range of this argument employ the metaphor of the game and the repetitive use of this metaphor is analyzed as emblematic of the era. It mirrors the *couleur du temps.* Docile and utile bodies are part of this *game of power* in which anarchy reigns. The figure of the universal individual is able to reflect the effects of power on man-as-body as well as on man-as-species.

The artists within the range of this argument depict *acts* and *emotions* that are 'ciphers searching for their meaning among the hard, chromium furniture of

381 {see Foucault, Society, pp. 242, 246, 247, 252, 253, 254, 256, 258}

382 {see Pasolini, Salò}

our minds.'[383] The quote from Ballard exemplifies the gulf or *lacune* between language and world that produces a split between statement and meaning. *Acts* and *emotions* have lost their referentiality and hence the search for meaning is endless. Tambling considers that allegory and personification work in opposite modes. Allegory stresses that surface meaning is not the ultimate quarry of interpretation whereas personification emphasizes the face that appears, i.e. the surface meaning.[384] It is argued that the surface meaning within the range of this discussion is impenetrable because the face itself is fragmented. Arctor who asks himself 'which of them is me' illustrates the loss of identity and thus there is no surface meaning. Allegory is not about understanding meaning but about *awe*. Its vagueness only empowers its affective quality. The analyzed allegories are invested in the deconstruction of Manichean aesthetics and do not follow static rules. « Jetons bas ce vieux plâtrage qui masque la façade de l'art! Il n'y a ni règles, ni modèles ; »[385] Craven, Watkins, Selby, Dick, Hasford and Romero are revolutionary in their approach to art and create strong works that are enigmatic. The *content* of their works as well as the *form* of their works are reinventing art. As they are mirrors to ideology they also follow no rules. Jameson describes Dick's work as "a virtual 'art of the fugue' of storytelling, narrative pyrotechnics that unravel themselves in delirium and can stand as a *critique of representation itself*."[386] All the works in this argument are based on the utopia of the very principle of equivalence and thus are a critique of representation itself.

The final remark of this argument is about the critical act. Dayan Stetco refers to Barthes in *The Crisis of Commentary* with regard to the critical act. Barthes outlines the plural constitutes the text and interpretation is an operation that is meant to appreciate the plural. He states criticism is not a science and wonders if the refusal of a creative streak is supposed to increase clarity. Stetco concludes that it is an illusion to assume the critical act can clarify anything. She is convinced it only increases the mystery and the plurality of the work. The refusal to mirror the creativity of fiction has a considerable side effect, which is the removal of the critical commentary from the primary source.[387] The aim of this argument is to create a connection to the primary source, some kind of um-

383 {see Ballard, Crash, p. 149}

384 {see Tambling, Allegory, pp.171, 173}

385 {see Hugo, Cromwell, p. 88. "Let us relieve art from the obsolete form that disguises it! There are no rules or models;" [trans. mine]}

386 {see Jameson, Archaeologies, p. 348}

387 {see Paula Willoquet-Maricondi and Mary Alemany-Galway, Peter Greenaway's Postmodern / Poststructuralist Cinema (Lanham 2008), pp. 203, 206}

bilical cord that nourishes the creation of a meaningful constellation or network. There is nothing to clarify, nothing to solve, as the works are unresolvable. Only the pure joy of a voyage through the ocean of language / images with the intention to praise the enigmatic quality of the works.

Additional Notes on Authors / Auteurs

Wes Craven

Wes Craven envisioned titles like *Sex Crime of the Century* or *Krug and Company* for his film *The Last House on the Left*. But unfortunately these titles were not inciting audiences to watch the film. Someone from PR recommended the title *The Last House on the Left* because 'last' and 'left' had an uncanny notion. Audiences responded to this title and thus it became the title of the film. Craven states the title does not have anything to do with the film. It is ironic that the title itself illustrates the gap between language and world.[388]

Other films by Wes Craven include *The Hills have Eyes* (1977), *A Nightmare on Elm Street* (1984), *The Serpent and the Rainbow* (1988), and *Scream* (1996).

Peter Watkins

Punishment Park was filmed in August 1970, in the San Bernadino desert. Peter Watkins's homepage states that since the release of *Punishment Park* in America the film has been shown rarely in cinemas and never on TV. The New York Times describes the film as 'the wish fulfilling dream of a masochist.' Rolling Stone voted *Punishment Park* one of the best films in 1971.[389]

Other films by Peter Watkins include *The War Game* (1965), *Gladiators* (1969), and *La Commune, Paris 1871* (2000).

Hubert Selby, Jr.

Darren Aronofsky made an adaptation of *Requiem for a Dream* in 2000. Selby and Aronofsky both worked on the screenplay and succeeded in translating the tone of the novel onto the screen. Here the *how* is crucial again as the montage and the film music (performed by the Kronos quartet) are an essential part of the films affective quality.

388 {see David Gregory, Celluloid Crime of the Century (USA 2003)}

389 {see http://pwatkins.mnsi.net/punishment.htm}

The documentary *Hubert Selby Jr: It/ll be better tomorrow* (2005) portrays Selby as an extraordinary writer who does not receive the praise for his work that he deserves.

His other works include *Last Exit to Brooklyn* (1964), *The Demon* (1976), *Requiem for a Dream* (1978), and *Songs of the Silent Snow* (1986).

Philip K. Dick

Philip K. Dick does not receive the same attention as Science Fiction writers like Isaac Asimov or Frank Herbert. Dick was a mostly-penniless writer and at times almost destitute.[390]

The director Richard Linklater adapted the novel *A Scanner Darkly* in 2006. Its visual innovative style translates the Science Fiction elements in the novel successfully onto the screen. But unfortunately the consumer criticism prevalent in the novel has been omitted in the film. Due to this omission the film cannot reach the social and historical dimension of the novel.

His other novels include *The Three Stigmata of Palmer Eldritch* (1965), *Do Androids Dream of Electric Sheep?* (1968), *Ubik* (1969), and *VALIS* (1980).

Gustav Hasford

Donald Ringnalda states that no writer had as much to say about America's collective delusion on the subject of the Vietnam War as Michael Herr.[391] His novel *Dispatches* is highly acclaimed and still in print. Gustav Hasford wrote three novels and none of them are in print at the moment. One of the outstanding talents of American literature is not accessible to a whole generation.

The adaptation of Hasford's novel *The Short-Timers* by Stanley Kubrick is a disappointment. *Full Metal Jacket* (1987) is a good film but it is not a good adaptation. The echo of Milos Forman can be heard saying 'make it real.' Joker's nightmarish visions of the green room, mechanical centaurs, vampires and ghouls are completely missing. Kubrick just *omitted* the tone of the novel.

His other novels are *The Phantom Blooper* (1990) and *A Gypsy Good Time* (1992).

---

390 {see Dick, Minority, p. ix}

391 {see Donald Ringnalda, Fighting and Writing: America' Vietnam War Literature (Apr. 1988), p. 29}

George A. Romero

In connection to the release of *Dawn of the Dead* are two release years circulating which are 1978 and 1979. The film was released in Europe in 1978 and in America in 1979. The American release is regarded as the date relevant for this discussion.

> The controversy surrounding *Dawn*, and its success worldwide, made me 'hot' again, though on a small scale. (I was only a 'cult' figure, after all; a mysterious guy who made movies in … where was it, Philadelphia?) I was happy. It looked like I was going to be able to keep working for a while. [392]

Dawn of the Dead is part of the Dead trilogy. The first part is *Night of the Living Dead* (1968) and the third part is *Day of the Dead* (1985). Romero continued to develop further his concept of tension between majority and minority. In *Dawn* a priest says in the beginning of the film that 'we must stop the killing or lose the war.'[393] This idea is taken to the next step in his film *Land of the Dead* (2005). The end of the film shows how humans and zombies are trying to find a way to live together without eating / killing the opposition.

Other films include *The Crazies* (1973), *Martin* (1976), and *Diary of the Dead* (2007).

392 {see Gagne, The Zombies, p. 101}
393 {see Romero, Dawn}

Works Cited

Primary Sources

Ballard, J. G. *Crash* (London: Harper Perennial, 2008).

Brecht, Bertolt. *Rise and fall of the City of Mahagonny* (London;, New York: Methuen Drama, 2007).

Brecht, Bertolt, Desmond I. Vesey, and Eric Bentley. *The Three Penny Opera* (New York: Grove Weidenfeld, 1964).

Burroughs, William. *The Soft Machine* (London: Corgi Books, 1970).

---. *Exterminator: A Novel* (New York: Penguin Books Ltd, 1979).

Craven, Wes. *The Last House on the Left.* (USA 1972).

Dick, Philip K. *Minority Report* (London: Gollancz, 2002).

---. *A Scanner Darkly* (New York: Vintage Books, 2006).

Hasford, Gustav. The Short-Timers (New York: Bantam Books, 1985).

Hugo, Victor, and Annie Ubersfeld. *Cromwell* (Paris: Flammarion, 1990).

Lucas, George. *THX 1138* (USA 1971)

Matheson, Richard. *I Am Legend* (London: Millennium, 1999).

Miller, Henry. *The World of Sex* (New York: Grove Press, Inc., 1965).

---. *The Colossus of Maroussi* (Middlesex: Penguin Books Ltd, 1967).

---. *The Obelisk Trilogy* (Paris: Olympiapress.com, 2004).

Pasolini, Pier Paolo, dir. *Salò o Le 120 Giornate di Sodoma.* (Italy 1975).

Priest, Christopher. *The Prestige* (London: Orion, 2006).

Romero, George A., Dir. *Dawn of the Dead. (USA* 1979).

Selby, Hubert. *Requiem for a Dream: A Novel* (New York: Thunder's Mouth Press, 2000).

---. *The Room* (London: Penguin, 2011).

Thompson, Hunter S. *Better than Sex: Confessions of a Political Junkie* (New York: Ballantine Books, 1995).

Thoreau, Henry D. *Civil Disobedience and other Essays* (New York: Dover Publications, 1993).

Vonnegut, Kurt. *Slaughter-House Five, or The children's Crusade: A Duty-Dance with Death* (New York: Dell, 1988).

---. *Breakfast of Champions: Or, Goodbye Blue Monday!* (New York: Dell, 1999).

Watkins, Peter, *Punishment Park* (USA 1970).

---. <http://pwatkins.mnsi.net/punishment.htm>, Web. 10 May 2012

Secondary Sources

Abrams, Meyer H. *A Glossary of Literary Terms* (Fort Worth, Tex: Harcourt Brace Jovanovich College Publ., 1992).

Althusser, Louis. *On Ideology* (London ;, New York: Verso, 2008).

Barot, Emmanuel. *Camera Politica: Dialectique du Réalisme dans le Cinéma Politique et Militant (Groupes Medvedkine, Francesco Rosi, Peter Watkins)* (Paris: J. Vrin, 2009).

Barthes, Roland. *Barthes: Selected Writings*. Ed. Susan Sontag ([London]: Fontana/Collins, 1983. Print.

Bastian, Dawn E., and Judy K. Mitchell. *Handbook of Native American Mythology* (Oxford ;, New York: Oxford University Press, 2008).

Baudrillard, Jean. *Amérique* (Paris: Grasset et Fasquelle, 1986).

---. *In the Shadow of the Silent Majorities* (Los Angeles, Cambridge, Mass: Semiotext(e); Distributed by MIT Press, op. 2007).

---. *Simulacra and Simulation* (Ann Arbor: University of Michigan Press, 1997).

Bertens, Hans. *Literary Theory: The Basics* (London: Routledge, 2001).

Cook, David A. *Lost Illusions: American Cinema in the Shadow of Watergate and Vietnam, 1970 - 1979* (Berkeley [u.a.]: Univ. of California Press, 2002).

Copeland, Rita, and Peter T. Struck. *The Cambridge Companion to Allegory* (Cambridge, UK;, New York: Cambridge University Press, 2010).

Courtine, Jean-François, Michel Deguy, and Éliane Escoubas. *Du Sublime* (Paris: Belin, DL 2009).

Cronenberg, David, Serge Grünberg, and Claudine Paquot. *David Cronenberg: Interviews with Serge Grünberg* (London: Plexus, 2006).

Cronenberg, David, and Chris Rodley. *Cronenberg on Cronenberg* (London: Faber and Faber, 1997).

Debord, Guy. *Society of the Spectacle* (Detroit: Black & Red, 1983).

Deleuze, Gilles. "*Postscript on the Societies of Control.*" *The MIT Press* Winter, 1992, Vol. 59: 3–7. Web. 24 Apr. 2012. <http://www.jstor.org/stable/778828>.

Du Gay, Paul, Jessica Evans, and Peter Redman. *Identity: A Reader* (London;, Thousand Oaks, Calif: SAGE Publications in association with The Open University, 2000).

Foucault, Michel. *Discipline and Punish: The Birth of the Prison* (New York: Vintage Books, 1995).

---. *"Society must be defended": Lectures at the Collège de France, 1975-76* (New York: Picador, 2003).

Freccero, Carla. "*Historical Violence, Censorship, and the Serial Killer: The Case of American Psycho.*" *Diacritics*, 2: 44–58. Web. 7 Mar. 2011. <http://jstor.org/stable/1566351>.

Gagne, Paul R. *The Zombies that ate Pittsburgh: The Films of George A. Romero* (New York: Dodd, Mead, 1987).

Gelder, Ken. *The Horror Reader* (London ;, New York: Routledge, 2000).

Giles, James R. *Understanding Hubert Selby, Jr* (Columbia, S.C: University of South Carolina Press, 1998).

Gottesman, Ronald. *Critical Essays on Henry Miller* (New York: Hall u.a., 1992).

Gregg, Melissa, and Gregory J. Seigworth. *The Affect Theory Reader* (Durham, NC: Duke University Press, 2010).

Gregory, David. *Celluloid Crime of the Century* (USA 2003)

Harris, Oliver. *William Burroughs and the Secret of Fascination* (Carbondale: Southern Illinois University Press, 2006).

Humphries, Reynold. *The American Horror Film: An Introduction* (Edinburgh: Edinburgh University Press, 2005).

Jameson, Fredric. *Archaeologies of the Future: The Desire called Utopia and other Science Fictions* (New York: Verso, 2007).

Kristeva, Julia. *Powers of Horror: An Essay on Abjection* (New York: Columbia University Press, 1982).

Kucukalic, Lejla. *Philip K. Dick: Canonical Writer of the Digital Age* (New York: Routledge, 2009).

Lacan, Jacques. *Die vier Grundbegriffe der Psychoanalyse* (Weinheim: Quadriga, 1987).

Marx, Karl, and David McLellan. *Selected Writings* (Oxford [Eng.]: Oxford University Press, 1977).

McLuhan, Marshall. *Understanding Media: The Extensions of Man* (London: Routledge, 2001, c1994).

Newton, Kenneth M. *Twentieth-Century Literary Theory: A Reader* (Basingstoke ;, London: MacMillan Education, 1988).

Pasolini, Pier P., Bernhart Schwenk, and Michael Semff. *P.P.P. Pier Paolo Pasolini and Death* (Ostfildern, New York: Hatje Cantz; D.A.P. [distributor], 2005).

Peers, William R., et al. *The My Lai Massacre and its Cover-Up: Beyond the Reach of Law?* (New York: Free Press, 1976).

Reeves, Richard. *President Nixon: Alone in the White House* (New York: Simon & Schuster, 2001).

Ringnalda, Donald. *Fighting and Writing: America's Vietnam War Literature* Journal of American Studies 22.1 (1988): 25–42. Web. 3 Mar. 2011. <http://www.jstor.org/stable/27554936>.

Sartre, Jean-Paul. *Colonialism and Neocolonialism* (London:, New York: Routledge, 2006).

Silliman, Stephen W. "*The "Old West" in the Middle East: U.S. Military Metaphors in Real and Imagined Indian Country.*" *American Anthropologist* 110.2 (2008): 237–47. Print.

Stam, Robert. *Film Theory: An Introduction* (Malden, MA: Blackwell, 2000).

Tambling, Jeremy. *Allegory* (New York: Routledge, 2010).

Webster's *New Encyclopedic Dictionary* (New York: Black Dog & Leventhal Publishers, 1995).

Willoquet-Maricondi, Paula, and Mary Alemany-Galway. *Peter Greenaway'Postmodern/Poststructuralist Cinema* (Lanham, Md: Scarecrow Press, 2008).

Table of Figures

Zeitfracht Medien GmbH
Ferdinand-Jühlke-Straße 7
99095 Erfurt, Deutschland
produktsicherheit@kolibri360.de